Breathing Never Felt So Much Like Dying

By: Travis Prino

Published by Travis Prino

Edited by Travis Prino

Copyright © 2007 by Travis Prino

All rights reserved. No part of this book may be reproduced or transmitted in any form or by any means without the written permission of the Publisher.

All poems written by and are the original work of Travis Prino Except "Lights And Sirens" Written by Travis Prino and Steve Westerfield

Cover Art by Sara Hubbell

Photograph by Hans Fischer

ISBN: 978-0-6151-4059-9

:o)

Table Of Contents

Title	Page #
Wasting Away	10
Skin Deep	12
Second Chances	14
With Or Without You	16
It's Over	19
Asking Why	21
Trust In Me	23
Find Me Here	25
Leaving This	28
Another Sleepless Night	30
So I'll Go	32
Your Savior	34
LifeLoveTrustFaith	36
Lost And Gone	39
Wither	42
Left Behind	44
Under Different Circumstances	46
Anything Or Everything	49
Guiding Light	51
Sincerely Me	53
The Great Divide Part 1: Mother Unkind	55
This Pain	57
Unknown	59
Graveside Where I Hide	61
In Your Head	63
Sometimes	65
Fighter	67
Control	69
Fighting With Shadows	72
Unravel	74
A Pact	77
Run Away	80

Title	Page #
Fade To Black	82
Pain Is Hunger	84
Don't Leave	86
Finding Me	88
Silence The Voices	90
I Remember	92
Tomorrow	94
Follow Me Down	96
Letting Go Of Misery	98
Dead Ends And Road Blocks	100
Sky Came Falling	102
Picture Frames And Melodies	104
Failure	106
Insignificant	108
Too Little Too Late	111
Summer Meets Winter	113
Love In A Photograph	115
Breaking Through	117
Disintegrate	119
Broken Down	121
Actions Defy Reasons	123
Bleeding You	125
Portrait	127
Counting Sheep	129
Stranger Am I	131
Road To Me	133
See Through	135
I'm Alright	137
Reason To Crawl	139
Severed Ties	141
Choke	143
I Lost You	145
Third Time's A Charm	147

Title	Page #
Distance Between (Another Day's Gone)	149
Burn	151
Take It All Away	153
Burgundy Bliss	155
Behind Closed Doors	157
This Is Me	159
3,000 Miles	161
Alone Again	163
Broken Soul	165
In Silence	167
Paintings On The Wall	169
Long Way Home	171
Haunt	174
Death To An Angel	176
The Great Divide Part 2: Faceless	177
Memories Remain	179
Porcelain	181
Breathless	183
A Plague Infects Us All	184
Crystal Ball	186
A Part Of Me…	188
Poison In My Mouth	190
So Tired	192
Home	194
I Miss You	196
Turn The Page	198
Is This Love?	200
Only Time	202
The Answers You Find Will Kill You	204
The Sound Of Silence	206
Starlit Sky	209
Across The World	211
Breaking Up Is The First Step Towards Recovery	213

Title	Page #
Failed Apologies	215
Time To Let Go	217
Fool For You	219
Tear Shed Roses	221
How Bitter Sweet Is	223
Dear September	224
Once And For All (Wake Up)	226
Say Hello To Loneliness	228
Sunsets Like Raindrops	230
The Hunger, The Rapture, The Toast	232
A River Red	234
Blanket Of Nothing	236
What Once Was Pure Now Is Tainted	239
Throwing Bricks In Glass Houses (Break Out)	241
Heaven's Calling	243
Phone Line To Your Heart	246
Lights And Sirens	249
Rescue You	251
A Dance With The Devil Can Only Leave You Dead	253
Cigarette Street Lights	256
You In The Ground Makes Perfect Sense	258
If Only I Could Wish You Away	260
Hatred In Our Eyes	262
A Killer In Me	265
Chances With Kisses	267
These Hands	269
Change Doesn't Always Come Easy	271

Dedications seem so trite

So I'm just gonna take this time to thank everyone who has supported me and encouraged me along the way

For never letting me give up and pushing me to finally see this through

It's been a long journey and hopefully this is not the end but only the beginning

So thank you

~ Trav ~

"WASTING AWAY"

Watching as the sun goes down
believing everything around
cringing cause I can not take the sound
moving forward up the creek
losing sight of what I seek
words are caught in my throat and I can't speak

wasting away
I feel it as my body trembles I'm
wasting away
my life feels like it's disassembled I'm
wasting away
and this is something that I can't handle I'm
wasting away
wasting away

pull myself together now
and get my life on track somehow
I never knew this world could be so loud
I started in the wrong direction
searching for someone's affection
now nothing looks the same in my own reflection

wasting away
I feel it as my body trembles I'm
wasting away
my life feels like it's disassembled I'm
wasting away
and this is something that I can't handle I'm
wasting away
wasting away

forgetting everything I know
all I have I'm letting go
hoping that this time I'll thrive and grow
looking back into my past
I realize it's fading fast
so I'll say goodbye and try to make this last

wasting away
I feel it as my body trembles I'm
wasting away
my life feels like it's disassembled I'm
wasting away
and this is something that I can't handle I'm
wasting away
wasting away

waiting for a brighter day
so that I can finally say
never again in my life will I feel this pain
finding that there's no escape
turn my sadness into hate
I've tried so hard but now it's just too late

wasting away
I feel it as my body trembles I'm
wasting away
my life feels like it's disassembled I'm
wasting away
and this is something that I can't handle I'm
wasting away
wasting away.

"SKIN DEEP"

You feel like hurting me tonight
but I will not put up a fight
and all this time will take it's toll
cause I've been losing all control
there's many battles won and lost
and they all leave me with a cost
my thoughts are stranded in my mind
my heart is racing all the time

if you look close enough you'll see
see me crawl beneath your skin
that thing you feel inside is me
I'm sinking deeper and deeper in
if you look close enough you'll see
see me crawl beneath your skin
that thing you feel inside is me
I'm sinking deeper and deeper in
I'm sinking deeper and deeper in

you look confused but so do I
cause this life stares us in the eye
and I don't know where I'll end up
I think for now I'll just stay stuck
so move along now on your way
don't think I will ask you to stay
cause I am through with all your shit
this time I won't put up with it

if you look close enough you'll see
see me crawl beneath your skin
that thing you feel inside is me
I'm sinking deeper and deeper in
if you look close enough you'll see
see me crawl beneath your skin
that thing you feel inside is me
I'm sinking deeper and deeper in
I'm sinking deeper and deeper in

you liked to always put me down
and knew that I would stick around
but this time isn't like the last
don't be so sure about the past
I've made mistakes that I've paid for
but now I'm walking out the door
goodbye is what I'll say to you
goodbye this much I know is true

if you look close enough you'll see
see me crawl beneath your skin
that thing you feel inside is me
I'm sinking deeper and deeper in
if you look close enough you'll see
see me crawl beneath your skin
that thing you feel inside is me
I'm sinking deeper and deeper in
I'm sinking deeper and deeper in
I'm sinking deeper and deeper in
I'm sinking deeper and deeper in

goodbye…..this much I know is true.

"SECOND CHANCE"

When I look into your eyes
it doesn't take much time
and it's then I realize
that I love you
you're the only one I adore
when we're together I feel secure
these thoughts and feelings I know for sure
are through and through

you are everything that matters
you are everything I need
you are everything that matters
that's why I'm begging please
you are everything that matters
you are everything I need
you are everything that matters
will you please forgive me?

I know I made a big mistake
and it brought us to this break
there's only so much I can take
without you near
I'm feeling selfish and absurd
there's many lessons left to be learned
but the fire in me still burns
wanting you here

you are everything that matters
you are everything I need
you are everything that matters
that's why I'm begging please
you are everything that matters
you are everything I need
you are everything that matters
will you please forgive me?

can we give this one last try?
please don't say this is goodbye
cause there's one star left in the sky
for us tonight
can we just start this over again?
you know we can't be just friends
cause neither of us can pretend
that we're alright

you are everything that matters
you are everything I need
you are everything that matters
that's why I'm begging please
you are everything that matters
you are everything I need
you are everything that matters
will you please forgive me?

will you please forgive me?
you just have to forgive me.

"WITH OR WITHOUT YOU"

I sit here dissatisfied
thinking of your face
there's something that I realize
we both are out of place
now I know where you belong
standing at my side
nothing left but I must be strong
cause you still aren't mine

with or without you
I'm losing my mind
with or without you
I'm running out of time
with or without you
it's driving me insane
with or without you
I'm dealing with this pain
with or without you

I look at you and fail to see
the secrets that you hold
the only thing that's clear to me
is all that I've been told
you seem so perfect in and out
I can not find a flaw
in my mind there is no doubt
the beauty that I saw

with or without you
I'm losing my mind
with or without you
I'm running out of time
with or without you
it's driving me insane
with or without you
I'm dealing with this pain
with or without you

I'm trying hard to understand
these feelings deep inside
it seems like love is in my hands
but all I do is hide
you're reaching out to give me hope
but still I can not see
the only thing to help me cope
is having you with me

with or without you
I'm losing my mind
with or without you
I'm running out of time
with or without you
it's driving me insane
with or without you
I'm dealing with this pain
with or without you

you found someone months ago
you've been with till this day
I just want to let you know
my heart is where you'll stay
you need to open up your eyes
to see me waiting here
before the chance I gave you dies
and I just disappear

with or without you
I'm losing my mind
with or without you
I'm running out of time
with or without you
it's driving me insane
with or without you
I'm dealing with this pain
with or without you.

"IT'S OVER"

Do you look at me the way I look at you?
I know something that you never knew
we've grown apart and I'll walk away
all this will come an unsuspecting day
you'll take it hard then you'll fall apart
but nothing you do will get you to my heart
all this time I spent by your side
was nothing more than just one big lie

it's over, it's over
I'm saying goodbye
it's over, it's over
just don't ask me why
it's over, it's over
your time here is gone
it's over, it's over
from this point on

you call me up and you want me back
you try so hard just to make me crack
you push and pull like this is a game
but deep inside we'll never be the same
you sound real sweet and so sincere
then you turn around and make it crystal clear
you say you love me then you act like a whore
it took a year and a half for me to even the score

it's over, it's over
I'm saying goodbye
it's over, it's over
just don't ask me why
it's over, it's over
your time here is gone
it's over, it's over
from this point on

I tried my best to make you understand
but you could never comprehend
so I'm leaving you for someone else
I hope your life is good in hell
cause you have no one left to blame
you brought it all on and now it came
I hope you know what you lost was true
I hope you know that I loved you

it's over, it's over
I'm saying goodbye
it's over, it's over
just don't ask me why
it's over, it's over
your time here is gone
it's over, it's over
from this point on

it's over, it's over
it's over, it's over
it's over, it's over
IT'S OVER.

"ASKING WHY"

Why does this pain always build up inside?
why can't this hurt go away for all time?
why am I left with so many questions?
why are there things that I can't even mention?
why do I feel like the world's growing stronger?
why do I feel I can't take this much longer?
why do I sit here and think of the past?
why is my life going by me so fast?

please tell me why
I've been left here to die
and now I cry
cause no one's by my side
please tell me why
my life has been a lie
and now I sigh
and choke on all my pride
please tell me…..why?

why does my mind play games with my heart?
why does it pick all the pieces apart?
why does my heart then play games with my mind?
why am I stuck in this world undefined?
why do I feel like I'm all by myself?
why doesn't anyone offer me help?
why is it so hard to find all the answers?
why was I brought to the world with this cancer?

please tell me why
I've been left here to die
and now I cry
cause no one's by my side
please tell me why
my life has been a lie
and now I sigh
and choke on all my pride
please tell me…..why?

why doesn't anyone know how I feel?
why is it so hard to know what is real?
why is it I'm always here on my own?
why can't I find the cure for alone?
why am I tormented by all these demons?
why is it no one can find me the reason?
why does it seem there is no other way?
why do I ask myself why everyday?

please tell me why
I've been left here to die
and now I cry
cause no one's by my side
please tell me why
my life has been a lie
and now I sigh
and choke on all my pride
please tell me…..why?

just tell me…..why?
now tell me…..why?
why…..why?

"TRUST IN ME"

Trust in me
and soon you'll see
everything that you can be
trust in me
and soon you'll see
how I'm gonna set you free

feel me under you at night
even though I'm out of sight
breathe me in and hold it tight
I'll bring you closer to the light
all the things you thought were real
are set in place just to conceal
and all the things you think you feel
will leave you on your own to heal

trust in me
and soon you'll see
everything that you can be
trust in me
and soon you'll see
how I'm gonna set you free

you see the sky it's turning gray
the darkness comes to claim it's prey
it sucks you in and there you'll stay
always night and never day
sit in silence as you wait
alone again to contemplate
change yourself or die with hate
there's time to reconstruct your fate

trust in me
and soon you'll see
everything that you can be
trust in me
and soon you'll see
how I'm gonna set you free

follow me into the sun
I'll lead you from the evil done
the world is full of choices to come
don't be led astray by some
all you need is to believe
more than what your mind conceives
it's easier just to deceive
but greater feats you can achieve

trust in me
and soon you'll see
everything that you can be
trust in me
and soon you'll see
how I'm gonna set you free.

"FIND ME HERE"

Find me here
there's nowhere else I'd rather be
right here waiting
till the day that you're with me
find me here
there's no one else that I can see
stop debating
follow your heart straight to me

you feel me there
even though I'm far away
you know I care
as lonely nights turn into days
your mind goes numb
you think out loud yet to yourself
it overcomes
you hate the hand that you've been dealt
you watch it all
from someone else's point of view
you might just fall
and forget about what you want to do

find me here
there's nowhere else I'd rather be
right here waiting
till the day that you're with me
find me here
there's no one else that I can see
stop debating
follow your heart straight to me

I feel the same
I want you when you're not around
still I feel lame
this love is felt without a sound
I think of you
wishing I could hold you tight
not much I can do
but sit alone and out of sight
I know you know
all the things that I feel inside
don't let go
I'll keep trying till the end of time

find me here
there's nowhere else I'd rather be
right here waiting
till the day that you're with me
find me here
there's no one else that I can see
stop debating
follow your heart straight to me

we won't give up
see this is worth fighting for
we just feel stuck
holding on to that something more
we'll try our best
to see if we can prove them wrong
we'll change this mess
into stable, healthy, strong
we will win
no matter what we must somehow
what we put in
will get us through the here and now

find me here
there's nowhere else I'd rather be
right here waiting
till the day that you're with me
find me here
there's no one else that I can see
stop debating
follow your heart straight to me.

"LEAVING THIS"

I'll catch a plane to Cali
maybe stop in Arizona
find a place to stay in Maui
while I'm drinking a Corona
I'll travel across the country
trying to find a home
and maybe if I'm lucky
I won't end up all alone

I'm leaving this place, this house, this life
I don't know where I'll end up tonight
but I'm leaving behind what got me here
I'm moving forward through all my fear

I'll find my way to South Dakota
or even Santa Fe
I could wind up in Georgia
and there I might just stay
I'll see a lot of places
all to me unknown
I'll see a lot of faces
but true colors are never shown

I'm leaving this place, this house, this life
I don't know where I'll end up tonight
but I'm leaving behind what got me here
I'm moving forward through all my fear

will I come apart in Texas
or stumble to Belize?
will I ever wake in Kansas
or fall asleep in The Keys?
I'll never know until I try
the world is calling me
I'm searching till the day I die
for somewhere I'll be happy

I'm leaving this place, this house, this life
I don't know where I'll end up tonight
but I'm leaving behind what got me here
I'm moving forward through all my fear

I'm leaving this place
I'm leaving this life
I'm leaving this place
and with it I'm leaving behind my fear.

"ANOTHER SLEEPLESS NIGHT"

He said "you know the air is cold at night"
she said "will it matter if I hold you tight?"
he said "I guess that it is plain to see"
she said "I know exactly what you mean"
he said "the problem lies in both of us"
she said "how can we get back the trust?"
he said "the question isn't how but why?"
she said "it never hurt before to try"

and they sit together but in separate homes
they finally realize what was once unknown
and as they sit together but in separate homes
they never felt so close, felt so alone

he said "it's getting late but I don't care"
she said "if you wanna go now don't you dare"
he said "I wouldn't even contemplate"
she said "just leave it in the hands of fate"
he said "how did all this get so bad?"
she said "somewhere we lost the spark we had"
he said "it doesn't have to be like this"
she said "forget the chances that we've missed"

and they sit together but in separate homes
they finally realize what was once unknown
and as they sit together but in separate homes
they never felt so close, felt so alone

he said "I still don't understand you know?"
she said "I think that it is best you go"
he said "tell me when I'll see you again"
she said "there's always time if we are friends"
he said "but don't you see that I want more?"
she said "you never really did before"
he said "the thought of you won't leave my mind"
she said "we're gonna have to give it time"

and they sit together but in separate homes
they finally realize what was once unknown
and as they sit together but in separate homes
they never felt so close, felt so alone

she never felt so close
he never felt so alone
she never felt so alone
he never felt so close
they never felt so close, felt so alone.

"SO I'LL GO"

Walking away from this pain deep inside
walking away to a place I can hide
walking away from these people I meet
walking away from this girl in defeat
crying alone with my head in my hands
crying alone cause I misunderstand
crying alone when I find out the truth
crying alone not knowing what to do

and I see it in your eyes
that you put on a disguise
and all the things that I've been told
are now starting to unfold
so when I walk away
you'll be begging me to stay
but you told me to let go
so I guess we'll never know

feeling ashamed of the things that I said
feeling ashamed waiting for the end
feeling ashamed, confused and bitter all the time
feeling ashamed I let you mess with my mind
turning my back on all that I feel
turning my back cause I just can't deal
turning my back though it is a mistake
turning my back from the hurt that you make

and I see it in your eyes
that you put on a disguise
and all the things that I've been told
are now starting to unfold
so when I walk away
you'll be begging me to stay
but you told me to let go
so I guess we'll never know

revisit the past to give it a go
revisit the past to learn what I didn't know
revisit the past to right all the wrongs
revisit the past, this won't take too long
all by myself struggling in my head
all by myself cursing all that I did
all by myself I'm starting anew
all by myself trying to forget you

and I see it in your eyes
that you put on a disguise
and all the things that I've been told
are now starting to unfold
so when I walk away
you'll be begging me to stay
but you told me to let go
so I guess we'll never know

so I'll go
I'll just go
let me go
so…I'll…go.

"YOUR SAVIOR"

Tell me what it is you need
tell me what it takes to bleed
cause I will show you all you want to see
and tell me what you really want
everything that can't be taught
cause I won't go until this war is fought
and tell me what you hold within
concealing underneath your skin
cause I won't let you live your life in sin

I'll be your savior
a pleasant sweet surprise
whenever you need more
just look up to the sky
I'll be your savior
a pleasant sweet surprise
whenever you need more
just look up to the sky
I'll be your savior

follow what is in your heart
you should've done it from the start
but I won't ever let you fall apart
remember everything I said
and how it all went to your head
so don't concede yourself to be misled
the world has got you by the throat
it's wrapped around you like a rope
but I'll be here whenever you can't cope

I'll be your savior
a pleasant sweet surprise
whenever you need more
just look up to the sky
I'll be your savior
a pleasant sweet surprise
whenever you need more
just look up to the sky
I'll be your savior

you question everything in life
you're moving farther from the light
but I will always make sure you're alright
your body's given up on you
you ask yourself what you can do
I'll show you things you thought were never true
you want your mind to be at ease
but you're so fucking hard to please
I'll be the one to pick you up off your knees

I'll be your savior
a pleasant sweet surprise
whenever you need more
just look up to the sky
I'll be your savior
a pleasant sweet surprise
whenever you need more
just look up to the sky
I'll be your savior

your savior.

"LIFELOVETRUSTFAITH"

Life
full of disease
infested with fleas
counting the time spent on your knees
begging for more
this game is a bore
you know who's on the other side of the door
hiding from you
but what can you do?
just leave them there with the choices they choose
and all that they take
still they never can break
what's inside, it's your only escape

I'm seeing for the first time what I haven't seen before
I'm seeing for the first time, I don't wanna see it anymore

Love
no more than a mess
it's nothing but stress
it leaves you cold at night undressed
with no one around
you sit on the ground
in silence as you wait for the sound
of anyone else
someone but yourself
to put the pieces back up on the shelf
that fell to the floor
right after the storm
that left you beaten, broken and sore

I'm seeing for the first time what I haven't seen before
I'm seeing for the first time, I don't wanna see it anymore

Trust
keeping you down
you lost what you found
you watch it leave you to the pound…
…ing of the clock
the tick and the tock
never believe that you're the cream of the crop
you'll always be wrong
you're singing a song
to tell everyone you wish that you were strong…
…ger than you are
but you've come this far
don't give up now cause it'll all fall apart

I'm seeing for the first time what I haven't seen before
I'm seeing for the first time, I don't wanna see it anymore

Faith
the only thing left
bullet in my chest
finding a way that I can rest
from all of this
I never will miss
all of the shit that brought me to bliss
now it is done
I don't need to run
everything's back to where it started from
far away from here
now I'm in the clear
beginning to notice there is nothing to fear

I'm seeing for the first time what I haven't seen before
I'm seeing for the first time, I don't wanna see it anymore
but show it to me just once more

these things have a way of fucking with you
don't think that's everything there's more you can do
just be patient and it won't be so bad
things will get better you won't always be sad

now show it to me just once more.

"LOST AND GONE"

Waiting
this time it's for you
hating
this feeling of blue
walking
to somewhere else
talking
but it never helps
changing
all the things that I've been
rearranging
cause I can't find my friend
feeling
the waves crashing down
kneeling
in these tears I will drown…drown…drown

you never had to go away
in my heart you had a place to stay
I think about you everyday…everyday…everyday
I'll see you in the future but
this can not come soon enough
I'm waiting just to feel your touch…your touch…your touch

hoping
to see the sun shine
coping
just trying to ease my mind
dreaming
while I'm awake
sleeping
just to escape
finding
there's no use at all
trying
to prepare for the fall
learning
I can't fight the pain
searching
for answers in vain…in vain…in vain

you never had to go away
in my heart you had a place to stay
I think about you everyday…everyday…everyday
I'll see you in the future but
this can not come soon enough
I'm waiting just to feel your touch…your touch…your touch

burning
my past in the fire
turning
a new leaf of desire
knowing
I'll never forget
growing
further than I ever meant
making
myself move on
faking
this somber calm
realizing
I will never learn
fantasizing
of your return…return…return

you never had to go away
in my heart you had a place to stay
I think about you everyday…everyday…everyday
I'll see you in the future but
this can not come soon enough
I'm waiting just to feel your touch…your touch…your touch.

"WITHER"

I need a lover
I need a friend
I run for cover
when I start to bend
I won't let it break me
I'll carry this through
I'll embrace reality
and hold what is true

I
wanna feel alive
I wanna touch the sky
believe I'll never die
and I
don't wanna crumble apart
don't want a broken heart
believe there's more than what we are

I need a guardian
I need a saint
I hide when the pain sets in
so my voice is faint
I'll bury it in my soul
so no one will stay
I do just like I was told
I wither away

I
wanna feel alive
I wanna touch the sky
believe I'll never die
and I
don't wanna crumble apart
don't want a broken heart
believe there's more than what we are

I need a leader
I need a pawn
I can do without either
I know right where I belong
I knew I would make it
nothing could keep me down
so don't be mistaken
all I've been looking for is found

I
wanna feel alive
I wanna touch the sky
believe I'll never die
and I
don't wanna crumble apart
don't want a broken heart
believe there's more than what we are

follow what's inside and it'll never be wrong
follow what's inside and you'll never go wrong
follow what's inside
inside

I
wanna feel alive
I wanna touch the sky
believe I'll never die
and I
don't wanna crumble apart
don't want a broken heart
believe there's more than what we are

foolish of you to think I'd wither away.

"LEFT BEHIND"

All you ever wanted from me
is right before your eyes
all you ever needed me to be
I hid behind these lies
all the things I never let you see
they still exist inside
all the things I said to set you free
I wish I could turn back time

I got left behind
thrown away
there's nothing more for me to say
I got left behind
you ran away
I need you more than ever today

all the times that you said "I love you"
I will never forget
I think of all the shit that we've been through
and all that's left is regret
I know you feel the same way I do
I must get you to admit
there's only room left in this world for two
somehow we seem to fit

I got left behind
thrown away
there's nothing more for me to say
I got left behind
you ran away
I need you more than ever today

you feel it's time for you to let go
I have to stop you somehow
too many things that you still don't know
you just can't leave right now
I need more time, the process is slow
but soon you'll figure out
without you here I live in sorrow
I just can't say it aloud

I got left behind
thrown away
there's nothing more for me to say
I got left behind
you ran away
I need you more than ever today

for everything I've ever done
this is my apology
for everything I've never done
this is my apology

I got left behind
thrown away
there's nothing more for me to say
I got left behind
you ran away
I need you more than ever today.

"UNDER DIFFERENT CIRCUMSTANCES"

I wonder how this life would be if I were someone else
would I take everything I own and leave it on the shelf?
there's more to life than what we know but will we ever find
the meaning we are looking for that is hidden so deep inside

I ask, I beg, I plead, I pray
cause I need more strength today
I ask, I beg, I plead, I pray
will someone guide me on my way?
I ask, I beg, I plead, I pray
cause I need more strength today
I ask, I beg, I plead, I pray
won't anyone come and show me the way?

I wonder how this life would be if it was seen through different eyes
would I turn and run away or would I give in to the lies?
the world is changing everyday, there is no turning back
despite our fear we must go on and plan our next attack

I ask, I beg, I plead, I pray
cause I need more strength today
I ask, I beg, I plead, I pray
will someone guide me on my way?
I ask, I beg, I plead, I pray
cause I need more strength today
I ask, I beg, I plead, I pray
won't anyone come and show me the way?

I wonder how this life would be if I walked in a stranger's shoes
would I win more than I do now or would I simply continue to lose?
these games we play are complicated and put us to the test
they leave us at the bottom trying to sort through all the mess

I ask, I beg, I plead, I pray
cause I need more strength today
I ask, I beg, I plead, I pray
will someone guide me on my way?
I ask, I beg, I plead, I pray
cause I need more strength today
I ask, I beg, I plead, I pray
won't anyone come and show me the way?

I wonder how this life would be if I were given one more chance
would I take it and finally make it or suffer the consequence?
the time we have is running out and can never be regained
the choices that we make from here on out we will carry to our graves

I ask, I beg, I plead, I pray
cause I need more strength today
I ask, I beg, I plead, I pray
will someone guide me on my way?
I ask, I beg, I plead, I pray
cause I need more strength today
I ask, I beg, I plead, I pray
won't anyone come and show me the way?

I wonder how this life would be
I wonder how this life could be
I wonder how this life will be
I wonder
and wonder

I ask, I beg, I plead, I pray
cause I need more strength today
I ask, I beg, I plead, I pray
will someone guide me on my way?
I ask, I beg, I plead, I pray
cause I need more strength today
I ask, I beg, I plead, I pray
won't anyone come and show me the way?

show me the way
give me strength today
cause I wonder.

"ANYTHING OR EVERYTHING"

You wanna know what I feel inside
you wanna see what it is I hide
you wanna put a bullet in my head
you wanna see me lying face down dead
you wanna play all the games we play
don't wanna do everything we say
you wanna throw caution to the wind
but it'll all come back to you in the end

you'll see that anything and everything is not the same
cause you'd give anything but I know I'd give everything
and now you're sitting there considering if I am sane
cause I'd give everything and you can't give me anything

I wanna know what it is you feel
want you to tell me is it truly real?
I wanna hear when your heart beat stops
I'll be the one to catch you when you drop
I wanna fall on your every word
don't want you to think that I am being absurd
I wanna die in your warm embrace
but I can't even seem to recognize your face

you'll see that anything and everything is not the same
cause you'd give anything but I know I'd give everything
and now you're sitting there considering if I am sane
cause I'd give everything and you can't give me anything

you wanna run far away from here
you wanna swim cause you're drowning in fear
you wanna lose everything we had
you wanna turn it all around and make it all look bad
you wanna start your life over again
but don't you see with time there is no way to pretend
you wanna finally see us through
but you will never forget the thought of me and you

you'll see that anything and everything is not the same
cause you'd give anything but I know I'd give everything
and now you're sitting there considering if I am sane
cause I'd give everything and you can't give me anything

I wanna make it all work out
wanna erase all those feelings of doubt
I wanna be here for a while
I wanna wait it out just so I can see you smile
I wanna fall down upon my knees
want you to know that I am still here begging please
I wanna give you everything you want
but I will show you a love that never can be bought

you'll see that anything and everything is not the same
cause you'd give anything but I know I'd give everything
and now you're sitting there considering if I am sane
cause I'd give everything and you can't give me anything.

"GUIDING LIGHT"

I sit alone and watch the days go by
up in my room I just wonder why
please tell me now what can I do?
cause I would do anything for you
I'm living in my own personal hell
wretched pain is the only thing I've felt

can you do me a favor?
can you stay with me tonight?
give me something to savor
won't you be my guiding light?

you're running through my head all day long
but from your mind lately I've been gone
now tell me where did all your love go?
I love you but I'm feeling so low
cause you don't love me anymore
and I am left here feeling insecure

can you do me a favor?
can you stay with me tonight?
give me something to savor
won't you be my guiding light?

all that's left now is my broken heart
I think of you and wish to go back to the start
now you're telling me that we're just friends
at this time the love between us ends
though my chances may seem real slim
I'll keep trying even if I can't win

can you do me a favor?
can you stay with me tonight?
give me something to savor
won't you be my guiding light?

you know that I love you
and even if you say that I won't do
that is something that will not change
I know the feelings you are feeling are strange
maybe in time we will be together
and if so maybe then it will be forever

can you do me a favor?
can you stay with me tonight?
give me something to savor
won't you be my guiding light?

"SINCERELY ME"

I sit alone all by myself
I try so hard to think of something else
but you are the only thing on my mind
thoughts of you are in my head all the time
I take a walk and I think of us
and wonder if what I'm feeling is lust
but I know that this isn't true
cause I know I'm in love with you

you use me
confuse me
abuse me so
you refuse me
you'll lose me
I just hope you know

I dream of you all day and night
and hope there is some way to make it all right
I just want to hold you in my arms
I'll try my best to protect you from harm
I cherish every second I see your face
I need to know the feel of your embrace
listen now to every word I say
and please stop trying to push me away

you use me
confuse me
abuse me so
you refuse me
you'll lose me
I just hope you know

I think you've got some feelings inside
that for some reason you are trying to hide
though I know that I could be wrong
I'll keep my head up and try to be strong
all I want is to give us a try
cause living without you rains tears from my eyes
I've told you before and I'll tell you again
I will never stop loving you…..not till the end

you use me
confuse me
abuse me so
you refuse me
you'll lose me
I just hope you know

so I'll sit alone all by myself
and I'll try to think of something else.

"THE GREAT DIVIDE PART 1: MOTHER UNKIND"

She walked away and turned her back
two boys and a husband left alone just like that
four years old not knowing what to do
with a six year old brother who was fucked up and confused
a man left alone with nowhere to turn
he must now raise a family but alone he must learn

you lied to us
misled our trust
what can you do?
nothing you're screwed
bred deep within
bled through our skin
you left, you're gone
goodbye, so long

tell me what did I do to make her go away?
tell me what can I do to have her back someday?
was it that I was too bad or just not good enough?
or was it that I was just not something she could love?
did I always cry too much or make too much noise?
it really shouldn't matter, you should've been there for your boys

you lied to us
misled our trust
what can you do?
nothing you're screwed
bred deep within
bled through our skin
you left, you're gone
goodbye, so long

she used to visit from time to time
I wish I could say that the pleasure was mine
but alcohol and cigarettes were the scent on her breath
and when it all hit me I knew the feeling of death
she drank too much and now it seems her life has passed her by
she missed out on the joy it'd bring to have her children by her side

you lied to us
misled our trust
what can you do?
nothing you're screwed
bred deep within
bled through our skin
you left, you're gone
goodbye, so long

thirteen years later and still on my own
no one there for comfort, nowhere to call my home
on this journey called life I have done my share of thinking
my anger's been building and I feel like I'm sinking
I will never forgive her not for all these years
no matter how hard I try I can never dry these tears

you lied to us
misled our trust
what can you do?
nothing you're screwed
bred deep within
bled through our skin
you left, you're gone
goodbye, so long.

"THIS PAIN"

My life feels like a derailed train
far from reality and close to insane
I look to the future but I don't see the light
all the choices I make are always wrong never right
I conjure up evil thoughts in my head
as I lie awake unable to sleep in my bed
what can I do to make the voices go away?
so I can open my eyes to see another day

this pain I've lived with for so long
this pain tells me I can't go on
this pain I've lived with for so long
this pain tells me I can't go on

I sit in silence knife in hand
these feelings and emotions I can no longer stand
the burning sensation starts to set in
as the blade cuts deeper into my skin
I try to stop but this will not be
my mind has lost all control of me
desire so intense it has turned to hate
there is nothing I can do, now it's too late

this pain I've lived with for so long
this pain tells me I can't go on
this pain I've lived with for so long
this pain tells me I can't go on

the blood drips down and falls to the floor
as my entire arm begins to feel sore
I clench my fist with a smile on my face
never could I imagine it would feel this great
I look at the wound, I am almost done
all that's left is the final cut
I will put an end to all my misery
with just one more swipe and at last be free

this pain I've lived with for so long
this pain tells me I can't go on
this pain I've lived with for so long
this pain tells me I can't go on

it brings me misery
won't ever let me be
but now I'm free
now I'm free
from this pain.

"UNKNOWN"

Your name to me is unknown
your face to me is unknown
you fail to see
what you can be
the world to you is unknown

your heart is in your hands
you take it like a man
all that's left and all that's gone
leaves you with your burdens shown
your mind is broken down
you've fallen to the ground
all you know and all you knew
has been forgotten much too soon

your name to me is unknown
your face to me is unknown
you fail to see
what you can be
the world to you is unknown

your eyes have lost their sight
darkness consumes the light
all you lost and all you gained
still it seems nothing remains
your body has lost touch
but you still feel the rush
quiet times creeping in
leaves you there without a friend

your name to me is unknown
your face to me is unknown
you fail to see
what you can be
the world to you is unknown

your love has been put to the test
they push and pull but they never rest
all you have and all you give
won't be enough in this world you live
your soul leads your life astray
it washes all your hopes and dreams away
you're giving up, you're burning out
learning the hard way the true meaning of doubt

your name to me is unknown
your face to me is unknown
you fail to see
what you can be
the world to you is unknown
everything is unknown.

"GRAVESIDE WHERE I HIDE"

I turn you on, I turn you off
I keep you breathing with a cough
make a wish upon a star
hear the endless beating of my heart
nothing ventured, nothing gained
I broke your will and you feel chained
bound and tied up on the floor
wrestling demons once more

never realized what she was worth
never appreciated what she gave
now I must live without it
now I must think about it
or so they say

I knock you down, I pick you up
I save your blood inside a cup
give it to you when you need
I love to sit and watch you bleed
pleasure flowing through my veins
when I see that you're in pain
will still broken in my hands
I'm the one you call your man

never realized what she was worth
never appreciated what she gave
now I must live without it
now I must think about it
or so they say

I love you dearly, I hate you
sick of the shit that you put me through
manipulation at it's best
you won't pass the final test
said you loved me but you lied
I'm the reason that you died
love so strong it was blind with fear
left with memories of blood, sweat and tears

never realized what she was worth
never appreciated what she gave
now I must live without it
now I must think about it
or so they say

now I live without it
but I don't think about it
as she lies in her grave.

"IN YOUR HEAD"

How could you turn your back on me?
you knew from the start that we were meant to be
how could you tell me that we're through?
being by yourself it isn't easy to do
how could you lie right to my face?
you told me all you needed was a little space

and did you think about everything before it was said?
did you think about it over and over again?
did you think about everything before it was said?
did you think about it over and over in your head?

how could you turn and run away?
everything is different at the end of the day
how could you change your mind just like that?
and leave it all behind at the drop of a hat
how could your heart be so cold?
you left before we ever had the chance to grow old

and did you think about everything before it was said?
did you think about it over and over again?
did you think about everything before it was said?
did you think about it over and over in your head?

how could you be so serious?
I know I set the fire that burned your trust
how could you give up so easily?
nothing that we've gained has ever come for free
how could you honestly let go?
cause my heart is breaking, thought I'd let you know

and did you think about everything before it was said?
did you think about it over and over again?
did you think about everything before it was said?
did you think about it over and over in your head?

you're making a big mistake
time is all it'll take
just think about it
think about it
you're making a big mistake
time is all it'll take
just think about it
think about it

and did you think about everything before it was said?
did you think about it over and over again?
did you think about everything before it was said?
did you think about it over and over in your head?

"SOMETIMES"

I feel the walls are closing in
it may be too late for me to begin
all the time that I spent here
I'm standing face to face with all my fear

    sometimes we have to let it go
    sometimes the pain begins to show
    sometimes we open up and grow
    sometimes, sometimes
    sometimes we have to let it go
    sometimes the pain begins to show
    sometimes we open up and grow
    sometimes, sometimes

blood flows up and down my spine
voices echoing through my mind
I've been taken from the place I know
and it's killing me from head to toe

    sometimes we have to let it go
    sometimes the pain begins to show
    sometimes we open up and grow
    sometimes, sometimes
    sometimes we have to let it go
    sometimes the pain begins to show
    sometimes we open up and grow
    sometimes, sometimes

I look ahead but I close my eyes
there's nothing there except gray skies
a future that's torn and a past that's gone
my present situation's all I'm thriving on

sometimes we have to let it go
sometimes the pain begins to show
sometimes we open up and grow
sometimes, sometimes
sometimes we have to let it go
sometimes the pain begins to show
sometimes we open up and grow
sometimes, sometimes

life is in your hands
so what are you gonna do?
life is in your hands
so what are you gonna do?
what are you gonna do?

sometimes we have to let it go
sometimes the pain begins to show
sometimes we open up and grow
sometimes, sometimes
sometimes we have to let it go
sometimes the pain begins to show
sometimes we open up and grow
sometimes, sometimes.

"FIGHTER"

I've been taken down
been lifted up for a second round
I've been done before
still you keep coming back for more
I've been on your side
seen all the pain and tears you've cried
I've been next to you
for all the shit you were going through

you make me
stand up and believe
faith in me
more than I can conceive
you break me
looks like I've been deceived
you rape me
down on my hands and knees
you bring out the fighter in me
the fighter in me

now it's round three
once again just you and me
now it's your turn
to know what it is to burn
now it's all gone
what we held so tight for so long
now it's memories
built around lies for centuries

you make me
stand up and believe
faith in me
more than I can conceive
you break me
looks like I've been deceived
you rape me
down on my hands and knees
you bring out the fighter in me
the fighter in me

round four is here
now it all seems so crystal clear
round four has passed
you watched it go by so slow yet so fast
round four bell rings
this is the end and new beginnings
round four is finished
like the flame that we extinguished

you make me
stand up and believe
faith in me
more than I can conceive
you break me
looks like I've been deceived
you rape me
down on my hands and knees
you bring out the fighter in me
the fighter in me

you brought out the fighter in me
now I'm a prize fighter.

"CONTROL"

I sit and wonder every day and night
so much to ponder, what is wrong and right
and now it's calmer cause you took the flight
well how much longer till we reunite?

defected
rejected
you took my heart and soul
congested
infested
my life is what you stole
and now I've lost control

I sit and think about the days of old
when we held each other in the cold
and this wasn't very long ago
still I'm waiting for you to come home

defected
rejected
you took my heart and soul
congested
infested
my life is what you stole
and now I've lost control

I sit and gather thoughts of me and you
you never realized that you left too soon
but now you're gone there's nothing I can do
all I asked was that you love me too

defected
rejected
you took my heart and soul
congested
infested
my life is what you stole
and now I've lost control

I sit and fancy what we could have been
do you even know what I'm feeling?
all I want is for the pain to end
the only way is for us to begin…..again

defected
rejected
you took my heart and soul
congested
infested
my life is what you stole
and now I've lost control

losing my mind
is this what you wanted?
lose track of time
nothingness, haunted
losing my mind
is this what you wanted?
lose track of time
nothingness, haunted

defected
rejected
you took my heart and soul
congested
infested
my life is what you stole
and now I've lost control

now you are in control.

"FIGHTING WITH SHADOWS"

I don't wanna fight anymore
cause we've been down this road too many times before
and I don't wanna wrestle the pain
cause all the joy in life has been taken away
I don't wanna leave us behind
cause what we had is something no one can find
and I don't wanna let it all go
cause what I've been feeling I can finally show

you were the one
you were my life
you were the one
the one I loved
you were the one
you were my life
you were the one
the one I loved

I don't wanna fight anymore
cause we've been down this road too many times before
and I don't wanna wrestle the pain
cause all the joy in life has been taken away
I don't wanna leave us behind
cause what we had is something no one can find
and I don't wanna let it all go
cause what I've been feeling I can finally show

you were the one
you were my life
you were the one
the one I loved
you were the one
you were my life
you were the one
the one I loved

I don't wanna love anymore
cause I've been down this road once before
I already wrestled the pain
in the end I lost all that I gained
now I've left us behind
time has shown me you were never mine
now I'll let it all go
it's much too late to let these feelings show

    you were the one
    you were my life
    you were the one
    the one I loved
    you were the one
    you were my life
    you were the one
    the one I loved

I don't know what to say
heart still broken today
I don't know what to say
my heart's still broken

    you were the one
    you were my life
    you were the one
    the one I loved
    you were the one
    you were my life
    you were the one
    the one I loved

you're still the one I love
but you have become
just shadows in my mind.

"UNRAVEL"

Watch me
I'm falling to pieces
you think that you know me but I don't listen to reason
watch me
I'm falling away from you
you think that you got me but I'm soaring without a clue
stop me
save me from dying
you already lost me, can you hear yourself crying?
stop me
catch me when I fall
you drop everything though you have nothing at all

cry yourself to sleep
cause you can't let it be
cry yourself to sleep
cause you're no longer with me
no longer with me

watch me
secretly from afar
you used to have me but you let it come apart
watch me
hopelessly wonder
you lie by yourself curled up under the covers
stop me
before I am gone
you want to hold me but you waited far too long
stop me
keep me from leaving
you do all you can you'll even keep me from breathing

cry yourself to sleep
cause you can't let it be
cry yourself to sleep
cause you're no longer with me
no longer with me

watch me
now that it's over
you thought you had me now you can't stay sober
watch me
continue to live my life
you tried to kill me but I slipped right through your vise
stop me
if only you could
you already tried failing always like you should
stop me
now cause we are through
you ruined it all so now I've ruined you

cry yourself to sleep
cause you can't let it be
cry yourself to sleep
cause you're no longer with me
no longer with me

became obsessed
turned into a mess
now you're on your own
became obsessed
turned into a mess
now you're on your own
and you unravel until you're gone

cry yourself to sleep
cause you can't let it be
cry yourself to sleep
cause you're no longer with me
no longer with me.

"A PACT"

I made a pact to stay the same
but nothing turned out that way
I told myself that you were wrong
but I'm just not that strong
in the end we made mistakes
pray to God that we don't break

      is it worth the fight?
      worth the crawl
      worth the night
      worth it all
      is it worth the fight?
      worth the crawl
      worth the night
      is it worth it all?

I made a pact to never change
but in your eyes it only stains
you told yourself you wouldn't run
now you're alone without the sun
only time can undo the past
pray to God this doesn't last

      is it worth the fight?
      worth the crawl
      worth the night
      worth it all
      is it worth the fight?
      worth the crawl
      worth the night
      is it worth it all?

I made a pact for me and you
to prove again that this love is true
I made a promise to both of us
but it disappeared in the lack of lust
we pulled together in those times of need
learning that it only made us bleed

is it worth the fight?
worth the crawl
worth the night
worth it all
is it worth the fight?
worth the crawl
worth the night
is it worth it all?

we tried so hard
we got this far
what's it all for?
we tried so hard
we got this far
what's it all for?

everything

is it worth the fight?
worth the crawl
worth the night
worth it all
is it worth the fight?
worth the crawl
worth the night
is it worth it all?

it's worth it all and more
it's worth everything.

"RUN AWAY"

I don't know where to go
it must be far away
so no one will know
all the mistakes that I've made
I'm packing a bag
getting ready to leave
there's not much I don't have
except my dignity, my dignity

I wanna run away to a place I can call home
run away from being tired and alone
run away to a place I can call home
run away, just run away

I'm feeling dumb and confused
I can't find my way out
broken from being abused
I'm underneath a dark cloud
my head is lost in a fog
I've got nowhere to turn
I used to run but I crawl
through ash of bridges I've burned, bridges I've burned

I wanna run away to a place I can call home
run away from being tired and alone
run away to a place I can call home
run away, just run away

the sun's shining down
beating upon my face
my smile turns to a frown
why am I such a disgrace?
I just wanna be free
from all the people around
the way they're looking at me
has burnt my will to the ground, will to the ground

I wanna run away to a place I can call home
run away from being tired and alone
run away to a place I can call home
run away, just run away

the way they look at me
I just want to be free
the way they look at me has burnt me down
it's burnt me down

I wanna run away to a place I can call home
run away from being tired and alone
run away to a place I can call home
run away, just run away
I wanna run away to a place I can call home
run away from being tired and alone
run away to a place I can call home
run away, just run away
run away, just run away.

"FADE TO BLACK"

She felt me run away from deep inside
I never let her see my feelings confined
she showed me how to love but I pushed her away
I never gave enough now she's gone today
and I'm in pain

I don't wanna be alone the rest of my life
I've given up any hope of feeling alive
the second I let her go it just passed me by
now I can't go back
watch it fade to black

she felt me run away even though I was there
within her broken heart she didn't know that I cared
she left me shivering out in the cold
now she'll never see all the secrets I hold
how I love her so

I don't wanna be alone the rest of my life
I've given up any hope of feeling alive
the second I let her go it just passed me by
now I can't go back
watch it fade to black

she felt me run away, she ran away herself
she didn't understand how she made me melt
I should've sucked it up and told her somehow
I never thought she would leave without a sound
and it's too late now

I don't wanna be alone the rest of my life
I've given up any hope of feeling alive
the second I let her go it just passed me by
now I can't go back
watch it fade to black

she's gone away but I'll be here
she's gone away but I'll be here
she's gone away but I'll be here
now and forever
now and forever

I don't wanna be alone the rest of my life
I've given up any hope of feeling alive
the second I let her go it just passed me by
now I can't go back
watch it fade to black

she felt me run away
now all I see is black.

"PAIN IS HUNGER"

He was hurting, pain inside
no one listened to this boy when he cried
she was hurting, feeling stuck
everybody knew but didn't give a fuck
he was losing, gone in stride
lack of attention now the years have died
she was falling out of luck
hate derived simply from a lack of love

it's not easy to see
how this life will be
when you're on your own
and you're all alone
but life goes on
life goes on

he graduated teacher's pet
he's almost out but he's not out yet
she was crying out for help
parents pretending that they couldn't tell
he's off to college, he won't forget
a family lost but no time for regret
she was failing in herself
trying to be a part of everyone else

it's not easy to see
how this life will be
when you're on your own
and you're all alone
but life goes on
life goes on

now he's married, gorgeous wife
you'd never realize he had such a hard life
she got addicted, fell apart
she couldn't take what had been done to her heart
his family distant but still alive
he'll never need them to be by his side
she's still breathing but full of scars
her family's gone she doesn't know where or who they are

it's not easy to see
how this life will be
when you're on your own
and you're all alone
but life goes on
life goes on
it's not easy to see
how this life will be
when you're on your own
and you're all alone
but life goes on
life goes on

pain is hunger
hunger thrives
ever wonder why the pain never dies?

"DON'T LEAVE"

You said that you were finally done
you said that you would never run
you need more time to get things straight
you said that you would sit back down
you said that you had lost your crown
you realize that you are what you hate

if you leave
please take me
cause without you
I'm nothing
if you leave
devastate me
cause I need you
to be something

you said that you had fucked up life
you said that you had to make it right
you didn't know that it's not in your hands
you said that it was best you leave
but I can almost guarantee
that won't solve anything in the end

if you leave
please take me
cause without you
I'm nothing
if you leave
devastate me
cause I need you
to be something

you said that you should go away
you said that this is not your place
you never knew the home that you had here
you said this was your last goodbye
you said it with tears in your eyes
I watched you go and didn't interfere

if you leave
please take me
cause without you
I'm nothing
if you leave
devastate me
cause I need you
to be something

we could have left together
no one would ever find us
we could have left together
our hearts will forever bind us
we could have left together
no one would ever find us
we could have left together
our hearts will forever bind us

if you leave
please take me
cause without you
I'm nothing
if you leave
devastate me
cause I need you
to be something.

"FINDING ME"

Holding on to flaring candles
letting go of nothingness
seeing what is unforgotten
exposing what is never said

finding me
lost somewhere else
hard to see
deep inside myself
finding me
lost somewhere else
hard to see
searching for help

uncovering my darkest secrets
showing what was left to me
revealing my own misconceptions
losing almost everything I need

finding me
lost somewhere else
hard to see
deep inside myself
finding me
lost somewhere else
hard to see
searching for help

looking for unanswered questions
following the circles in my head
getting back to where I started
giving up a part of me again

finding me
lost somewhere else
hard to see
deep inside myself
finding me
lost somewhere else
hard to see
searching for help

if I fall away
will you catch me?
if I fall away
will you catch me then?
if I fall away
will you catch me?
if I fall today
what then?

finding me
lost somewhere else
hard to see
deep inside myself
finding me
lost somewhere else
hard to see
searching for help

so will you catch me?
if I fall

"SILENCE THE VOICES"

Feeling dirty
so frustrated
don't you worry
soon you'll be sedated
lacking wisdom
failing truth
built upon suspicion
without the proof

lose yourself
away from home
go where no one's ever been before
forget yourself
you're so far gone
where no one's ever been before

falling backward
stupid feet
tripping forward
over what you can't see
flying higher
than a kite
don't put out the fire
it's our only light

lose yourself
away from home
go where no one's ever been before
forget yourself
you're so far gone
where no one's ever been before

feeble questions
you have your answers
watch deception
slowly entrance her
ticking time bomb
making noises
simple outcome
to right your wrong choices

lose yourself
away from home
go where no one's ever been before
forget yourself
you're so far gone
where no one's ever been before

before, before, before
where no one's ever been
before, before, before
where no one's ever been before
as you try to silence the voices.

"I REMEMBER"

I put on my shoes
I stepped out the door
I've got nothing to lose
what am I searching for?
I got in my car
I drove off today
will it tear us apart?
I guess we'll have to see

do you remember
the love we built together?
do you even remember
the love we shared together?
cause I remember
and I'll never forget her

I packed my bag
a hug and kiss goodbye
why does she look so sad?
why did I make her cry?
I think of all the good times
it brings me to tears
I think of all the bad times
wish I could fix all those broken years

do you remember
the love we built together?
do you even remember
the love we shared together?
cause I remember
and I'll never forget her

I broke her fragile heart
when I walked away
I miss being a part
of her every day
I've come to find
a love I didn't know
I'm drained and empty inside
never should've let her go

do you remember
the love we built together?
do you even remember
the love we shared together?
cause I remember
and I'll never forget her

in the end I hope I find her
in a place where the sun shines brighter.

"TOMORROW"

I'm lost in a sea of loneliness
I'm stuck in a web of confusion
I never thought that I would miss
the essence of your delusions
harder to breathe as the seconds pass
the air's diminishing
hoping my next breath won't be my last
what will tomorrow bring?

waiting it out
consumed in the here and now
waiting it out
longing for signs that will show me how
waiting it out
consumed in the here and now
waiting it out
longing for signs that will show me how

I'm fading faster in a cloud of dust
my senses all but gone
searching drastically for someone to trust
still I'm searching on my own
I never wanted it to be this way
with all the hurt and suffering
everything I am will soon decay
what will tomorrow bring?

waiting it out
consumed in the here and now
waiting it out
longing for signs that will show me how
waiting it out
consumed in the here and now
waiting it out
longing for signs that will show me how

I'm trapped in a cage of scrutiny
with all the accusations made
all the shit that was pinned on me
there's only so much I can take
I wish life was the way it was
before all the pain and aching
living to the fullest with your love
what will tomorrow bring?

waiting it out
consumed in the here and now
waiting it out
longing for signs that will show me how
waiting it out
consumed in the here and now
waiting it out
longing for signs that will show me how

you never know what's gonna happen
make the best with what you have
you never know what's gonna happen
make the best with what you have
you never know what's gonna happen
or what tomorrow may bring

waiting it out
consumed in the here and now
waiting it out
longing for signs that will show me how
waiting it out
consumed in the here and now
waiting it out
longing for signs that will show me how

I'm waiting…..waiting…..it out.

"FOLLOW ME DOWN"

You see the light it's bright ahead
you never listened to a word I said
you see the light it's burning out
take your chances and make this count

follow me down
I'm waiting for you
sorrow I found
a feeling brand new
follow me down
I'm waiting for you
hollow the sound
you never broke through

you see the future it's growing dim
you see the story coming to an end
the dream is over you've lost it all
brace yourself you're going to fall

follow me down
I'm waiting for you
sorrow I found
a feeling brand new
follow me down
I'm waiting for you
hollow the sound
you never broke through

you see the past so how'd it come to this
everybody always made you feel like shit
the game has just begun now you're in control
it's your turn time to take back what they stole

follow me down
I'm waiting for you
sorrow I found
a feeling brand new
follow me down
I'm waiting for you
hollow the sound
you never broke through
follow me down
I'm waiting for you
sorrow I found
a feeling brand new
follow me down
I'm waiting for you
hollow the sound
you never broke through

so follow…..follow…..me down.

"LETTING GO OF MISERY"

I'm letting go of misery
I'm trying to find a better way
looking for what I've never seen
I'll figure it out someday
and that's when I'll find
all of the answers
to all the questions
that I need answered

moving on ain't easy
it ain't easy to do
moving on ain't easy
it ain't easy without you
I'm bleeding from the inside out
I'm gonna see this through
erasing every inch of doubt
let the soul searching ensue

I'm letting go of misery
I'm trying to find a better way
looking for what I've never seen
I'll figure it out someday
and that's when I'll find
all of the answers
to all the questions
that I need answered

living life on my own
there's an aching in my heart
living life on my own
I wonder why we're apart
there is no way to prolong
feelings left behind so far
so I'll write it in a love song
and cast it off on a shooting star

I'm letting go of misery
I'm trying to find a better way
looking for what I've never seen
I'll figure it out someday
and that's when I'll find
all of the answers
to all the questions
that I need answered

I gotta let go if I'm gonna survive
I gotta let go just to feel alive
I gotta let go if I'm gonna survive
I gotta let go just to feel alive
so I'm letting go
letting go
I'm letting go of misery

I'll write it in a love song
and cast it off on a shooting star
hoping that one day it'll find you.

"DEAD ENDS AND ROAD BLOCKS"

Riddles unanswered leaving me puzzled
dead ends and road blocks in the way of my struggle
nowhere to turn in this maze of emptiness
feeling the burn of life's secrets I've missed
soon I'll be running out of time
crossing over to the other side

wash your hands
free of all the dirt and filth
in between the best of man
watch tranquility
change the color of our hearts
from red of rose to black and diseased
and then you'll find what's inside
then you'll find it all

beating me down so I'm left here with nothing
asking anyone just to show me something
something that I have yet to see
something that somehow has eluded me
soon you will witness me falling apart
soon you will witness the breaking of my heart

wash your hands
free of all the dirt and filth
in between the best of man
watch tranquility
change the color of our hearts
from red of rose to black and diseased
and then you'll find what's inside
then you'll find it all

look at me into my eyes
look at me through my disguise
look at me into my eyes
look at me through my disguise
look at me to see what you must find

wash your hands
free of all the dirt and filth
in between the best of man
watch tranquility
change the color of our hearts
from red of rose to black and diseased
and then you'll find what's inside
then you'll find it all.

"SKY CAME FALLING"

No one knows
what it's like
to be trapped in a hell you created (FOR YOURSELF)
and no one knows
what it's like
to live inside a mind that's depleted (BY YOURSELF)
the world keeps turning
time keeps ticking
nothing stays the same
light becomes darker
slowly sinking farther
it all remains unchanged

in a world so gray
you never see the day
cause the sky came crashing down (CRASHING DOWN)
in a world so gray
you never see the day
the sky came falling down (FALLING DOWN)

no one knows
what it's like
to feel the ascension of this depression (IN YOURSELF)
and no one knows
what it's like
to finally be free of all this tension (ON YOURSELF)
blackness consumes it
an unnatural lift
tightening it's grasp
covered in anger
becoming a stranger
to what is now the past

in a world so gray
you never see the day
cause the sky came crashing down (CRASHING DOWN)
in a world so gray
you never see the day
the sky came falling down (FALLING DOWN)

no one knows
what it's like
no one knows
what it's like
no one knows
what it's like
to see the sky come down
to watch the sky come down
but I do

in a world so gray
you never see the day
cause the sky came crashing down (CRASHING DOWN)
in a world so gray
you never see the day
the sky came falling down (FALLING DOWN)

the sky came crashing down
the sky came crashing down
the sky came falling.

"PICTURE FRAMES AND MELODIES"

Once upon a time…..

back in the day
before everything was gray
there was just me and you
we had a vision
a dumb superstition
that we would be together forever
I was so stupid
deep down I knew it
she would be gone real soon

picture frames tell the stories
of a life that used to be
and melodies play softly
but the words we still need to create
picture frames tell the stories
of a life that used to be
and melodies play softly
but the words we still need to create

do you remember the time
we watched the stars shine?
we were so untouchable
now things are different
how could I expect
we would grow so far apart?
now you're with someone
and I'm left with no one
how did it come to be like this?

picture frames tell the stories
of a life that used to be
and melodies play softly
but the words we still need to create
picture frames tell the stories
of a life that used to be
and melodies play softly
but the words we still need to create

you left me waiting
but you have taken
you left me waiting
but you have taken
you left me waiting
but you have taken
too long

picture frames tell the stories
of a life that used to be
and melodies play softly
but the words we still need to create
picture frames tell the stories
of a life that used to be
and melodies play softly
but the words we still need to create

so come back and play for me
come back and play for me.

"FAILURE"

Father forgive me
for all the times I've disappointed you
I'll never be what you want me to be
and nothing I do is ever good enough for you
so father forgive me
cause this time I'm following my dreams

I never wanted to be a failure
I'm just trying to make things better for everyone
I never wanted to be a failure
I'm stuck in between the pressure and the pain

mother forgive me
for all the times that I have hurt you
I never meant for it to be this way
but I pushed you so far that we wound up apart
so mother forgive me
cause this time I'm actually leaving

I never wanted to be a failure
I'm just trying to make things better for everyone
I never wanted to be a failure
I'm stuck in between the pressure and the pain

brother forgive me
for all the times that I wasn't there for you
I've never tried so hard for anything in life
but somehow I lost control and left you out in the cold
so brother forgive me
cause this time you get the best of me

I never wanted to be a failure
I'm just trying to make things better for everyone
I never wanted to be a failure
I'm stuck in between the pressure and the pain

this marks the beginning of the end
and the end of the beginning
this marks the beginning of the end
and the end of the beginning
this marks the beginning of the end
and the end of the beginning
this marks the beginning of the end
and the end of the beginning

I never wanted to be a failure
I'm just trying to make things better for everyone
I never wanted to be a failure
I'm stuck in between the pressure and the pain

feel the pain drive
you insane
feel the pain drive
you insane now.

"INSIGNIFICANT"

Reminiscing on the days I was falling through the cracks
thinking about all the times I was bending over backwards
now that is all but gone I can see it in your face
it's time to retrace and finally replace you

the way you
play all the games that you play
and say all the things that you say
you leave me struggling
you bring me tumbling
down to the ground at your feet
searching for words I can't speak
you broke my heart again
when will this ever end?
you make me feel so insignificant
you make me feel so insignificant
you make me (MAKE ME)
feel so (FEEL SO)
in…sig…ni…ficant (INSIGNIFICANT)

making believe that you are still here by my side
walking next to me down this winding road
but I know that's nothing more than a faint memory
of you and me and how it used to be back then

the way you
play all the games that you play
and say all the things that you say
you leave me struggling
you bring me tumbling
down to the ground at your feet
searching for words I can't speak
you broke my heart again
when will this ever end?
you make me feel so insignificant
you make me feel so insignificant
you make me (MAKE ME)
feel so (FEEL SO)
in…sig…ni…ficant (INSIGNIFICANT)

I had to let you go all you did was bring me down
you sucked the life out of me like an old forgotten flower
though I miss you more and more since the day you've been gone
it's time to move on so this is the last song for you

the way you
play all the games that you play
and say all the things that you say
you leave me struggling
you bring me tumbling
down to the ground at your feet
searching for words I can't speak
you broke my heart again
when will this ever end?
you make me feel so insignificant
you make me feel so insignificant
you make me (MAKE ME)
feel so (FEEL SO)
in…sig…ni…ficant (INSIGNIFICANT)

why do you treat me like this?
why do you make me cry?
why do you treat me like this?
why do you make me cry?
why do you treat me like this?
why do you make me cry?
well now it's your turn
it's your turn
it's your turn to cry

the way you
play all the games that you play
and say all the things that you say
you leave me struggling
you bring me tumbling
down to the ground at your feet
searching for words I can't speak
you broke my heart again
when will this ever end?
you make me feel so insignificant
you make me feel so insignificant
you make me (MAKE ME)
feel so (FEEL SO)
in…sig…ni…ficant (INSIGNIFICANT).

"TOO LITTLE TOO LATE"

You see the candle burning out
you think you know what I'm all about
you see the flame is growing dim
but you always wanted me to be him

    and now that it's over
    you're calling my name
    now that it's over
    you can't stay away
    and now that it's over
    you're calling my name
    so sorry to tell you
    it's too little too late

you see the water running dry
cause I have no more tears left to cry
you see our love flow down the drain
was your new pleasure worth all the pain?

    and now that it's over
    you're calling my name
    now that it's over
    you can't stay away
    and now that it's over
    you're calling my name
    so sorry to tell you
    it's too little too late

you see my light glowing again
without you my life doesn't have to end
you see your light fading to black
without me there you lost all that you had

and now that it's over
you're calling my name
now that it's over
you can't stay away
and now that it's over
you're calling my name
so sorry to tell you
it's too little too late

it's too little too late
you threw it all away
it's too little too late
you threw it all away
it's too little too late
you threw it all away
you'll never get it back
you'll never get me back
I'm never coming back to you.

"SUMMER MEETS WINTER"

Questions placed before me
with the answers undefined
how did you become to me
an image so divine?
holding on to something
that was lost so long ago
reasoning with demons
that are deep within my soul

you are the wind that blows
you are the crisp of the air
you are the summer rain
you are the white winter snow
you are the dark of night
you are the light of the day
you are the vibrant one
you are what keeps me here
and it makes me wonder why

I lost you a time ago
I can't remember when
I lost more than a lover
I lost my greatest friend
you made me feel important
you made me want to shine
but somehow I lost you
and now I don't feel alive

you are the wind that blows
you are the crisp of the air
you are the summer rain
you are the white winter snow
you are the dark of night
you are the light of the day
you are the vibrant one
you are what keeps me here
and it makes me wanna die

I haven't forgotten you
I think about you everyday
the thought alone it keeps me going
there is nothing I can't face
I know someday you'll be right here
though you think that you are strong
you'll be back here beside me
right back where you belong

you are the wind that blows
you are the crisp of the air
you are the summer rain
you are the white winter snow
you are the dark of night
you are the light of the day
you are the vibrant one
you are what keeps me here
and it makes me wanna try

so now I'm forever waiting for you.

"LOVE IN A PHOTOGRAPH"

You came to my house late last night
the lights were out cause I wasn't home
you waited at the door for me
did you really expect me to forgive you?
for all the games that you have played
that always end up the same

now I miss you
this time I miss you

you called me on the phone today
I didn't answer so you left me a message
you cried for me to call you back, to take you back
but I'm so sick of the same old shit
that you put me through for oh so long
I'll wave goodbye as I sing you this song

but now I miss you
this time I miss you

I put away the photographs
I've burned all of your stuff
I'm finding out the hard way
that love is not enough
this is the end of something beautiful
this is the end
the end of you and me

this is our last goodbye
though I may regret it
I'm never gonna feel this way again
this is our last goodbye
though I may regret it
I'm never gonna feel this way again
I'm never gonna feel this way again
so this is our last goodbye

I put away the photographs
I've burned all of your stuff
I'm finding out the hard way
that love is not enough
this is the end of something beautiful
this is the end
the end of you and me
I put away the photographs
I've burned all of your stuff
I'm finding out the hard way
that love is not enough
this is the end of something beautiful
this is the end
the end of you and me

now I miss you
this time I miss you.

"BREAKING THROUGH"

Tonight
you live inside of me
you taste the air I breathe
you tore my heart out of my chest
so fight
it's all that you have left
to justify this mess
that you made here so selfishly

this time I will not let you down
this time I'm breaking through
this time I have to let you down
this time I'm breaking through
I'm breaking through from you

tonight
your heart is beating fast
you thought that we would last
you played around now I am gone
so cry
cause you are all alone
you can't be on your own
you're now a part of my dying past

this time I will not let you down
this time I'm breaking through
this time I have to let you down
this time I'm breaking through
I'm breaking through from you

the door is locked you can't come in
the door is locked you can't come in
the door is locked you can't come in
so start again

this time I will not let you down
this time I'm breaking through
this time I have to let you down
this time I'm breaking through
I'm breaking through from you

you're left with only you
cause I'm breaking through from you
this time
next time
every time
all the time
for the rest of time
you have only you
cause I'm breaking through.

"DISINTEGRATE"

You come to me at night
in dreams I have to fight
to keep out of my head
while I'm lying in bed
you come to me at night
not in dreams but within my sight
to take me far away
so with you I will remain

you are the life inside my world
the captain of my ship
the best friend I've ever had
the answer to my tears
my picture perfect girl
the taste left on my lips
a love so good it's bad
the only thing that holds me close enough to take away my fear

you came to me today
but you disintegrate
the way you always do
when I'm holding onto you
you came to me today
with intention to make
me fall asleep forever
so that we could be together

you are the life inside my world
the captain of my ship
the best friend I've ever had
the answer to my tears
my picture perfect girl
the taste left on my lips
a love so good it's bad
the only thing that holds me close enough to take away my fear

everyday I dream of you
every night I dream of you
all the time I think of you
every moment my mind's on you
everyday I dream of you
every night I dream of you
all the time I think of you
every moment my heart's with you

you are the life inside my world
the captain of my ship
the best friend I've ever had
the answer to my tears
my picture perfect girl
the taste left on my lips
a love so good it's bad
the only thing that holds me close enough to take away my fear.

"BROKEN DOWN"

The first time is the last time
that I will ever need you here
and this time is my time
to make this situation clear

I don't want you
I don't need you
there is no easy way out
so get going
it was good knowing you
you finally got me broken down

so I'm leaving and you're grieving
what the hell happened to us?
and you're crying but I'm driving
we couldn't figure out what the problem was

I don't want you
I don't need you
there is no easy way out
so get going
it was good knowing you
you finally got me broken down

I'm gone now, you're alone somehow
you finally get what you deserve
cause I'm happy and you're unhappy
you finally get to feel the hurt

I don't want you
I don't need you
there is no easy way out
so get going
it was good knowing you
you finally got me broken down

no more goodbyes
no more next times
no more goodbyes tonight
no more goodbyes
no more next times
no more goodbyes tonight
no more goodbyes
no more next times
cause this is the last time that I will love you
this is the last time I will love you
this is the last time cause I'm broken down.

"ACTIONS DEFY REASONS"

Emphatically speaking
you can be everything to me
but I'm still bleeding
and so are you

so are you gonna be everything
that I want you to be?
so are you gonna be everything
that I want you to be?
so are you?

frustrated to see
you push away everything in me
but I'm still breathing
and so are you

so are you gonna be everything
that I want you to be?
so are you gonna be everything
that I want you to be?
so are you?

I guess it's too late
to put back the pieces
I guess it's too late
you're breaking my heart
breaking my heart
I guess it's too late
to put back the pieces
I guess it's too late
we're falling apart
falling apart
it's never too late
to put back the pieces
it's never too late
rewind to the start
rewind to the start
it's never too late
to put back the pieces
it's never too late
it's never too late

so are you gonna be everything
that I want you to be?
so are you gonna be everything
that I want you to be?
so are you?

you can be everything to me.

"BLEEDING YOU"

Where did you go?
cause I cannot find you
where did you go?
cause I can not find you
you left me alone
see my pain bleeding through
you left me alone
see my pain bleeding through

was it something I said?
was it something I did?
was it easier to just leave me here?
was it everything
that you thought it'd be?
was it easier to just leave me here?

where did you go?
cause I cannot find you
where did you go?
cause I can not find you
you left me alone
see my pain bleeding through
you left me alone
see my pain bleeding through

was it what you want?
was it what you got?
was it easier to just say goodbye?
and was it anything
that you thought it'd be?
was it easier to just say goodbye?

where did you go?
cause I cannot find you
where did you go?
cause I can not find you
you left me alone
see my pain bleeding through
you left me alone
see my pain bleeding through

in time I've wiped the blood away
but I could never make you stay
in time I've wiped the blood away
but I could never make you stay
in time I've wiped the blood away
but I could never make you stay
in time I've wiped the blood away
but I could never make you stay
and I will never be the same

where did you go?
cause I cannot find you
where did you go?
cause I can not find you
you left me alone
see my pain bleeding through
you left me alone
see my pain bleeding through

see me bleeding you.

"PORTRAIT"

I'm walking away from the havoc you create
cause you leave me no choice when you drown out my voice
with your incompetent words that sound so absurd
and I'm leaving behind the existence I called my life

        take me away
        someone, anyone
        take me away
        someone, anyone
        take me away
        someone, anyone
        and if not today
        then maybe tomorrow

I'm walking alone past the place we called our home
and now I'm breaking down wondering what you're doing now
are you with somebody else filling all the gaps you felt?
when I walked out on you but I'm the one left melancholy blue

        take me away
        someone, anyone
        take me away
        someone, anyone
        take me away
        someone, anyone
        and if not today
        then maybe tomorrow

I'm walking no more secretly silently longing for
this rope around my neck to bring me to my end
so all the suffering will cease to feel like anything
and all the blood I shed will paint my final portrait red

take me away
someone, anyone
take me away
someone, anyone
take me away
someone, anyone
and if not today
then maybe tomorrow

maybe it'll be alright
maybe I should die tonight
maybe it'll be alright
maybe I should die tonight
maybe it'll be alright
maybe I'll just die.

"COUNTING SHEEP"

The duller the knife
the harder the strike
it will leave me bloody and scarred
but it's just beginning
your voice is singing
I won't feel anything at all

the pain I feel inside it cuts me deep
like razorblades killing my counted sheep
and I'd do anything, anything, anything for sleep
and I'd give anything, anything, anything to sleep
to sleep it all away

the more I think
the more I sink
it's an endless cycle in my head
try to climb out
beaten down with doubt
better off motionless in my bed

the pain I feel inside it cuts me deep
like razorblades killing my counted sheep
and I'd do anything, anything, anything for sleep
and I'd give anything, anything, anything to sleep
to sleep it all away

ugly on the outside
to show of my insides
everyone will know this is your fault
bleed all that I've been
so much for not giving in
I'm dying here from this fatal assault

the pain I feel inside it cuts me deep
like razorblades killing my counted sheep
and I'd do anything, anything, anything for sleep
and I'd give anything, anything, anything to sleep
to sleep it all away

I wanna sleep it all away
sleep it all away
I wanna sleep it all away
sleep it all away
I wanna sleep forever
sleep forever
I wanna sleep forever
sleep forever

so I can forget her.

"STRANGER AM I"

I hate the way they look at me
the way they always stare
in one ear and out the other
but I can't say I don't care
suck it up and walk away
I'm so much bigger than that
bury it within myself
someday it'll all come back
I can't hold it in forever

I'm a stranger in my own skin
because of the way you treat me
I'm actually just like you
what can I do to make you see?
I'm a stranger in my own skin
because of the way you treat me
I'm actually just like you
why can't you see?

how they differentiate
the way I feel inside
from the way they feel for me
I see hatred in their eyes
but hatred stirs inside me too
they think we are so different
one thing that they've overlooked
we are one in the same consistent
I'm just trying to make things better

I'm a stranger in my own skin
because of the way you treat me
I'm actually just like you
what can I do to make you see?
I'm a stranger in my own skin
because of the way you treat me
I'm actually just like you
why can't you see?

you are what you hate
that's why you hate me
you are what you hate
that's why you hate me
you are what you hate
that's why you hate me
you are what you hate
that's why you hate me
but I hate you too

I'm a stranger in my own skin
because of the way you treat me
I'm actually just like you
what can I do to make you see?
I'm a stranger in my own skin
because of the way you treat me
I'm actually just like you
why can't you see?

a stranger am I?

"ROAD TO ME"

Is she gone (is she gone)?
gone forever (gone forever)
or is she simply on a road right back to me (back to me)?
is she gone (is she gone)?
gone forever (gone forever)
or is she simply on a road right back to me (back to me)?

I'm losing
sight of what I feel
everything that's real is crumbling down
I'm choosing
to finally let her go
but I don't even know if I want to now
and I'm boozing
to drown out all the pain
send my longing down the drain somehow

is she gone (is she gone)?
gone forever (gone forever)
or is she simply on a road right back to me (back to me)?
is she gone (is she gone)?
gone forever (gone forever)
or is she simply on a road right back to me (back to me)?

I'm pushing
to keep myself alive
but somehow this knife is in my hand
the cushion
that was my best friend
stabbed me in the back again, I don't understand
the solution
your name engraved in my wrist
it was quite the bloody mess, was this your plan?

is she gone (is she gone)?
gone forever (gone forever)
or is she simply on a road right back to me (back to me)?
is she gone (is she gone)?
gone forever (gone forever)
or is she simply on a road right back to me (back to me)?

was this your plan?
for me to die alone.

"SEE THROUGH"

Play my heart cause it's made this way
I've given in to every stupid thing you say
I don't ever wanna end up like you
I don't ever wanna be so see through
I see through you
I see through you
finally letting it all hang out
I'm sick and tired of your degrading mouth
you're breaking me into a million pieces
give it time I have a million reasons

you're fading right in front of me
I'm drowning you out of my mind
you're fading right in front of me
I'm drowning you out of my mind
you're fading right in front of me
I'm drowning you out of my mind
you're fading right in front of me
I wish I could drown you out of this life

play my heart cause it's made like this
I'm always giving in to your sultry kiss
I don't ever wanna do that again
I don't ever wanna live for the end
finally putting it all behind
nothing but deceit when I look in your eyes
I don't ever wanna end up with you
I never wanted you to be so see through
I see through you
I see through you

you're fading right in front of me
I'm drowning you out of my mind
you're fading right in front of me
I'm drowning you out of my mind
you're fading right in front of me
I'm drowning you out of my mind
you're fading right in front of me
I wish I could drown you out of this life

how could you fuck this up?
how could you fuck so much?
how could you throw it all away just to be a dirty slut?
how could you fuck this up?
how could you fuck so much?
how could you throw it all away just to be a dirty slut?

you're fading right in front of me
I'm drowning you out of my mind
you're fading right in front of me
I'm drowning you out of my mind
you're fading right in front of me
I'm drowning you out of my mind
you're fading right in front of me
I wish I could drown you out of this life

I saw through you
but I couldn't stop you
from killing me.

"I'M ALRIGHT"

I can tell by the look in your eyes
you didn't mean what you said
what you said the other night
and I feel fine
I can tell by the sound of your voice
you didn't wanna leave
you didn't have a choice
but I'm still fine
I'm still fine

I'm alright with you leaving me
I'm alright though I'm still bleeding
I'm alright with you leaving me
I'm alright, I can still hear you breathing
as if you're still here next to me

I can tell by the smell of your hair
you didn't wanna say goodbye
you wanted me to know you cared
now I'm just fine
I can tell by the way that you move
you didn't wanna walk away
you still had something to prove
but I am fine
I am fine

I'm alright with you leaving me
I'm alright though I'm still bleeding
I'm alright with you leaving me
I'm alright, I can still hear you breathing
as if you're still here next to me

I'm alright
I'll be fine
I'm alright
I'll be fine
I'm alright
I'll be fine
I'm alright
I'll be fine

I'm alright with you leaving me
I'm alright though I'm still bleeding
I'm alright with you leaving me
I'm alright, I can still hear you breathing
as if you're still here next to me

and even though you left
my heart you kept.

"REASON TO CRAWL"

You sleep where sun doesn't shine
how does it feel to be blind?
in the hole that you made for yourself
to everything to everyone else

isolated, separated
you've become so, so jaded
in a world you despised
you crawled away to a place you could hide
all the feelings of rejection
built up to resentment
they eat at you and your soul
you crawled away to a place of your own

you wake with no one around
alone is what you have found
to be the meaning of your life
like a gift you're wrapped up so tight

isolated, separated
you've become so, so jaded
in a world you despised
you crawled away to a place you could hide
all the feelings of rejection
built up to resentment
they eat at you and your soul
you crawled away to place of your own

you live your life in a box
enclosed to only your thoughts
of happiness brought by seclusion
making your dreams your illusions

isolated, separated
you've become so, so jaded
in a world you despised
you crawled away to a place you could hide
all the feelings of rejection
built up to resentment
they eat at you and your soul
you crawled away to a place of your own

you feel nothing at all
you are prepared for the fall
you found a reason to crawl
a reason to crawl
you feel nothing at all
you are prepared for the fall
you found a reason to crawl
a reason to crawl.

"SEVERED TIES"

Do you see what I see?
the colors are mixed together
and it's blurring my vision
but I keep a picture of you
in my head for all time
so I'll never forget your face

all the times that you said you loved me, you lied
and all the times that you walked out on me, I cried
all the times that you said you loved me, you lied
and all the times that you walked out on me, I cried
and it's plain to see that you weren't meant for me
it's plain to see that you weren't meant for me
so this is goodbye
and I'll dry my eyes
with these severed ties
with these severed ties

did you hear what I heard?
it's the tearing of our seams
that were holding us together
now they are all but gone
cause I can never forgive you
but I'll never forget your face

all the times that you said you loved me, you lied
and all the times that you walked out on me, I cried
all the times that you said you loved me, you lied
and all the times that you walked out on me, I cried
and it's plain to see that you weren't meant for me
it's plain to see that you weren't meant for me
so this is goodbye
and I'll dry my eyes
with these severed ties
with these severed ties

can you feel what I feel?
blood is pouring from my broken heart
and it's leaving me breathless
I used to know you so well
how could you do this to me?
and how did I forget your face?

all the times that you said you loved me, you lied
and all the times that you walked out on me, I cried
all the times that you said you loved me, you lied
and all the times that you walked out on me, I cried
and it's plain to see that you weren't meant for me
it's plain to see that you weren't meant for me
so this is goodbye
and I'll dry my eyes
with these severed ties
with these severed ties.

"CHOKE"

Take a look outside my window
and try to find yourself a rainbow
but the colors bleed into the sky
like you bleed into my eyes
like you bleed into my eyes

shattered glass and my heart in pieces
like the promises you broke
take this time to pick up the mess you made
hold your breath until you choke

take a look inside my bedroom
and try to find a piece of you
but the remnants of us don't exist
like all we had and all we missed
like all we had and all we missed

shattered glass and my heart in pieces
like the promises you broke
take this time to pick up the mess you made
hold your breath until you choke

you were nothing more
than one big lie
I hope you die
and you were nothing more
than just a fuck
your time is up
you were nothing more
than one big lie
I hope you die
and you were nothing more
than just a fuck
your time is up
SO DIE
SO DIE
SO DIE

shattered glass and my heart in pieces
like the promises you broke
take this time to pick up the mess you made
hold your breath until you choke
shattered glass and my heart in pieces
like the promises you broke
take this time to pick up the mess you made
hold your breath until you choke
and die
and die
and die.

"I LOST YOU"

I don't ever wanna see myself through your eyes
I don't ever wanna see through your disguise
this world was made for us
but I lost you
I lost you
I don't ever wanna see myself through your eyes
I don't ever wanna see all that you hide
this world was taken from us
I lost you
yeah I lost you

today is the last of all my days
today is the first of my days
today is the last of all my days
today is the first of my days
my days without you

I don't ever wanna see myself through your eyes
I don't ever wanna see through your disguise
this world was made for us
but I lost you
I lost you
I don't ever wanna see myself through your eyes
I don't ever wanna see all that you hide
this world was taken from us
I lost you
yeah I lost you

today is the last of all my days
today is the first of my days
today is the last of all my days
today is the first of my days
my days without you

now that you're gone
I will be strong
till you're in my arms
however long
now that you're gone
I will be strong
till you're in my arms
however long

today is the last of all my days
today is the first of my days
today is the last of all my days
today is the first of my days
my days without you.

"THIRD TIME'S A CHARM"

I thought of you the day she went away
it reminded me of the pain
that you brought into my life
but I wish that I could hold you in my arms tonight
I thought of you the day she broke my heart
it reminded me of your departure
the way you left me out in the cold
how you left me wondering, feeling so alone

somebody kill me
put a bullet in my head
I'll show you what it's like to bleed
we can do it over again
somebody kill me
put a bullet in my head
I'll show you what it's like to bleed
we can do it over again

I think of you although the years have passed
going over how I could have made it last
but you're not here and I can't see your face
my blood will drain until I'm gone from this place
I think of you because you were my first love
and since you left me I've been feeling so numb
it reoccurs with every girl I meet
an endless cycle started by your deceit

somebody kill me
put a bullet in my head
I'll show you what it's like to bleed
we can do it over again
somebody kill me
put a bullet in my head
I'll show you what it's like to bleed
we can do it over again

one time broken hearted
two times been discarded
third time's a charm I never wanted
one time broken hearted
two times been discarded
third time's a charm I never wanted

SO SOMEBODY KILL ME
PUT A BULLET IN MY HEAD
I'LL SHOW YOU WHAT IT'S LIKE TO BLEED
WE CAN DO IT OVER AGAIN
somebody kill me
put a bullet in my head
I'll show you what it's like to bleed
we can do it over again

we can do it over again
we can do it over again
we can do it over again
we can do it over again.

"DISTANCE BETWEEN (ANOTHER DAY'S GONE)

With every day that goes by
I feel you're drifting farther and farther away
see the sunlight dripping through my window as you awake
I feel complete but separated by this
I feel together but intoxicated by this
when will we know?
we can't let this go
we won't let this go

and now what about the distance that we have built between us
it catapults our senses into the deepest of lust
we held each other through the pain that was cast upon us
but nothing here can stop the rain as it drenches our intentions
and we watch it all slip away
and we watch it all slip away

with every night that passes
I feel you're slipping through my fingers
see the moonlight dripping through my window as I linger
I feel pathetic but defenseless by this
I feel important but I'm worthless by this
when will we show?
we want this to grow
we need this to grow

and now what about the distance that we have built between us
it catapults our senses into the deepest of lust
we held each other through the pain that was cast upon us
but nothing here can stop the rain as it drenches our intentions
and we watch it all slip away
and we watch it all slip away

another day's gone
it's been so long
since I've seen you smile
another day's gone
it's been so long
since I've seen you smile

and now what about the distance that we have built between us
it catapults our senses into the deepest of lust
we held each other through the pain that was cast upon us
but nothing here can stop the rain as it drenches our intentions
and we watch it all slip away
and we watch it all slip away.

"BURN"

I can't breathe with your hands around my neck
did you really expect me to believe you?
well I believed you and now I'm dead
from the words you said
you broke me down
you burnt me out

we can't even be friends anymore
it's escalated to a point of no return
we can't even be friends anymore
it's escalated to a point of no return
and I have burned
now I will burn for you

I can't see with this fire in my eyes
I remember the night that you said you were leaving
well it killed me and now I'm dead
from the words you said
they didn't make a sound
but they burnt me out

we can't even be friends anymore
it's escalated to a point of no return
we can't even be friends anymore
it's escalated to a point of no return
and I have burned
now I will burn for you

I'll drink this gasoline
so pure and so pristine
light a match and watch me burn
I'll drink this gasoline
so pure and so pristine
light a match and watch me BURN
I'LL BURN FOR YOU
ALL FOR YOU
CAUSE OF YOU
I BURN
I'LL BURN FOR YOU
ALL FOR YOU
CAUSE OF YOU
I BURN

we can't even be friends anymore
it's escalated to a point of no return
we can't even be friends anymore
it's escalated to a point of no return
and I have burned
now I will burn for you

now I burn cause of you.

"TAKE IT ALL AWAY"

Can you feel me breathing?
I'm lying next to you
but you don't even notice me
and my lungs still burn
but you can't hear me screaming
screaming your name at the sky

    you take it all away
    you broke my heart in two
    why do I still love you?
    you take it all away
    you broke my heart in two
    why do I still love you?
I hate myself for ever loving you

    can you feel the freezing?
    it's turning me to ice
when did you become so cold?
and my arms still hurt
but you can't feel me squeezing
holding onto you so tight

    you take it all away
    you broke my heart in two
    why do I still love you?
    you take it all away
    you broke my heart in two
    why do I still love you?
I hate myself for ever loving you

when you run for cover from the things you used to feel
there's nothing I can do or say to make your wounds heal
any faster, what a disaster we've become

you take it all away
you broke my heart in two
why do I still love you?
you take it all away
you broke my heart in two
why do I still love you?
I hate myself for ever loving you

when you run for cover from the things you used to feel
there's nothing I can do or say to make your wounds heal
any faster, what a disaster we've become.

"BURGUNDY BLISS"

You said that you would never hurt me
but I'm lying in a pool of my own blood
that I spilt for you
that was spilt for you
and every word you say's misleading
but the silence cuts me like a razor
I would kill for you
I'd kill myself for you

we never let these feelings show
we never gave ourselves the chance to grow
and I'm dying in this burgundy bliss
for the love of blood I'll take this out on my wrists

you said that you would never hurt me
but I'm calling out your name to no avail
in the dead of night
I am dead tonight
and every word you say's misleading
but the voices tell me I am not alone
when the morning comes
see what you have done

we never let these feelings show
we never gave ourselves the chance to grow
and I'm dying in this burgundy bliss
for the love of blood I'll take this out on my wrists

this heart is beating so hard to keep me alive
but it's not working anymore
what have you done to me?
what have I done to myself?
this pain never goes away
it will never go away

we never let these feelings show
we never gave ourselves the chance to grow
and I'm dying in this burgundy bliss
for the love of blood I'll take this out on my wrists

and everything will finally go away.

"BEHIND CLOSED DOORS"

My heart bleeds but you can't see
all that you've done to me
on this long night I'll hold on tight
hoping you will touch me just right
and your warm skin, I feel it again
underneath the blankets in my bed
your moist lips and your sweet kiss
are the reason I won't forget this

I know, I know what you're keeping inside
you know, you know all the feelings you hide
behind closed doors in front of you
I'll knock them down it's all I can do
to be with you

my head aches and I can't take
all the times you make my heart break
but on this night you are all mine
we will share a moment divine
cause I'm shaking and you're shaking
this is more than love we're making
and your body against my body
we're soaking wet but we're not stopping

I know, I know what you're keeping inside
you know, you know all the feelings you hide
behind closed doors in front of you
I'll knock them down it's all I can do
to be with you

to see your face sends a shiver down my spine
to hear your voice brings a twinkle to my eye
to feel your warmth makes me feel like I'm alive
I just want to hear you say those three words to me tonight
to see your face sends a shiver down my spine
to hear your voice brings a twinkle to my eye
to feel your warmth makes me feel like I'm alive
I just want to hear you say those three words to me tonight

I know, I know what you're keeping inside
you know, you know all the feelings you hide
behind closed doors in front of you
I'll knock them down it's all I can do
to be with you

to be with you
to be with you
cause I love you
do you love me too?

"THIS IS ME"

Your first impression doesn't seem quite fair
I'm waiting patiently for you here
the silence turned to darkness since you've been gone
can you hear me SCREAMING you this song

this is me
from the skin to the blood I bleed
this is me
screaming "darling don't you ever leave"
this is me
from the skin to the blood I bleed
this is me
screaming "baby, please don't ever leave"

I'm drunk again longing to touch your face
just don't believe all the things that they say
the truth only lies within my soul
I'm different now I thought you would've known

this is me
from the skin to the blood I bleed
this is me
screaming "darling don't you ever leave"
this is me
from the skin to the blood I bleed
this is me
screaming "baby, please don't ever leave"

the road ahead will leave me black and blue
don't you see it's taking me from you?
I just don't understand why you must leave
beneath the surface there is more to me

this is me
from the skin to the blood I bleed
this is me
screaming "darling don't you ever leave"
this is me
from the skin to the blood I bleed
this is me
screaming "baby, please don't ever leave."

"3,000 MILES"

Another endless night begins
thinking of you
how we used to be good friends
but what did I do?
now you've gone away
so far away
and I can't see you

3,000 miles apart
but you're still so close to my heart
with nothing in between
but street signs so misleading
3,000 miles apart
but you're still so close to my heart
with nothing in between
but street signs
leading me back to you

another day where the sun didn't shine
thinking of you
remembering when you could've been mine
but what did I do?
how we got to be so close
oh so close
then I lost you

3,000 miles apart
but you're still so close to my heart
with nothing in between
but street signs so misleading
3,000 miles apart
but you're still so close to my heart
with nothing in between
but street signs
leading me back to you

looking up into the sky
wonder if you see the same as I
looking up into the sky
wonder if you see the same as I
looking up into the sky
wonder if you see the same as I
looking up into the sky
wonder if you see the same as I
looking up, looking up

3,000 miles apart
but you're still so close to my heart
with nothing in between
but street signs so misleading
3,000 miles apart
but you're still so close to my heart
with nothing in between
but street signs
leading me back to you.

"ALONE AGAIN"

I'm sitting at home all alone again
I'm wondering all this time where you've been
I just need something to ease my mind
but you are the answer that I can not find

come and save me
come and take me away
to a place where everything will be okay
come and save me
come and take me away
to a time when I will finally hear you say
you're sorry

I'm walking home all alone again
I'm thinking about all the things you said
I just need something to dry my tears
but you are the reason for all my fears

come and save me
come and take me away
to a place where everything will be okay
come and save me
come and take me away
to a time when I will finally hear you say
you're sorry

I'm dying at home I'm alone again
you left me broken from all you did
I needed you just to cure myself
but you were the cause to the pain I felt

come and save me
come and take me away
to a place where everything will be okay
come and save me
come and take me away
to a time when I will finally hear you say
you're sorry

timing is everything
and I still mean nothing to you
if timing is everything
then why don't I mean anything to you?
timing is everything
and I still mean nothing to you
if timing is everything
then why don't I mean anything to you?
timing is everything
but I still mean nothing

come and save me
come and take me away
to a place where everything will be okay
come and save me
come and take me away
to a time when I will finally hear you say
you're sorry.

"BROKEN SOUL"

I feel alone again tonight
with only loneliness holding me tight
but these dreams swim inside my head
making me wish I was dead
till my blood is flowing red
I will suffer
I feel alone again inside
grasping to hold onto my life
but I've been hurting for so long
the pain I feel is just too strong
it won't cease until I'm gone
I will suffer

and this time all the pressure takes it's toll
on my mind, this adventure takes control
was doing fine now I remember a broken soul
that left me alone
that led me to alone

I feel alone again confined
so no one hears me when I cry
but this is more than I can take
it won't stop until I break
leaving me with my mistakes
I will suffer

and this time all the pressure takes it's toll
on my mind, this adventure takes control
was doing fine now I remember a broken soul
that left me alone
that led me to alone

I was doing fine
remembering makes me cry
can't someone help me save my life?
I was doing fine
remembering makes me cry
can't someone help me save my life?

and this time all the pressure takes it's toll
on my mind, this adventure takes control
was doing fine now I remember a broken soul
that left me alone
that led me to alone

I'm tired of being alone
I'll never be alone again
I'm tired of being alone
I'll never be alone again
I'll never be alone again
I'll never be alone again
with my new
red
friend.

"IN SILENCE"

You were my angel in disguise
and you opened up my eyes
the world brought us to our demise
now I am so alone
it seems you brought me to this place
these feelings I can not mistake
it all came crashing in my face
and I am on my own

in silence I slowly drift away
the things I feel I will never say
I guess we're better off that way
in silence I creep into the dark
you'll never know what's inside my heart
we'll live our lives two separate worlds apart
in silence your face it fades away

you left me hanging by a string
kept me blind with the pain you bring
held me close underneath your wing
so I'd never grow
then you dropped me like a wrecking ball
watched me stumble but I will not fall
you'd like me dead but I'm standing tall
now that I've let go

in silence I slowly drift away
the things I feel I will never say
I guess we're better off that way
in silence I creep into the dark
you'll never know what's inside my heart
we'll live our lives two separate worlds apart
in silence your face it fades away

I never loved anything more
but you tore my heart out
and left me to bleed
and bleed I did
till I was numb from
the way you made me feel
I never loved anything more
but you tore my heart out
and left me to bleed
and bleed I did
till I was numb from
the way you made me feel

in silence I slowly drift away
the things I feel I will never say
I guess we're better off that way
in silence I creep into the dark
you'll never know what's inside my heart
we'll live our lives two separate worlds apart
in silence your face it fades away

it will fade away forever.

"PAINTINGS ON THE WALL"

You see the picture in colors
but I see only black and white
you were the only one who really knew me
but I'm in the dark again tonight
and these paintings they can tell a story
of the life that you never knew
what happened to such an innocent boy?
a past I wish I shared with you

paintings on the wall
they can tell it all
leaving you with broken chains
paintings on the wall
they will tell it all
binding you to my remains

you see my face through a filter
that I wear to hide my scars
you always thought that you really knew me
you got so close but slipped incredibly far
and you only see what I will show
cause this mirror shelters me from you
an image that seems so immaculate
covering with lies all of the truth

paintings on the wall
they can tell it all
leaving you with broken chains
paintings on the wall
they will tell it all
binding you to my remains

how long will it be
till you see
the real side of me?
how long will it be
till you see
the real side of me?
not soon enough
not soon enough

paintings on the wall
they can tell it all
leaving you with broken chains
paintings on the wall
they will tell it all
binding you to my remains

these paintings they can tell a story.

"LONG WAY HOME"

You're on a high
all the time
waiting for the day you die
take this needle
that you feel
from your body till you keel
to the pain
in your veins
reinvigorate your brain
cause it's a long way home

you always feel the weight of the world
resting (RESTING) on your shoulders
you come to this place to escape
but you're wasting (WASTING) so far away
you look in the mirror and you don't like what you see
cause you're faking (FAKING) everything
but you're in too deep and there is no way out
cause you're addicted (ADDICTED) and should be dead by now

you're on a high
all the time
waiting for the day you die
take this needle
that you feel
from your body till you keel
to the pain
in your veins
reinvigorate your brain
cause it's a long way home

you always held the world by the neck
choking (CHOKING) it with your regrets
you find your answers in a liquid form
but you're dying (DYING) for something more
you reach for help but you recoil within
and you're lying (LYING) to yourself again
and the end approaches faster now
cause you're destined (DESTINED) to drown

you're on a high
all the time
waiting for the day you die
take this needle
that you feel
from your body till you keel
to the pain
in your veins
reinvigorate your brain
cause it's a long way home

you always blamed everyone else
but yourself
cause you were selfish
you always blamed everyone else
but yourself
cause you were selfish
now it's time to take responsibility
for your actions
time to kick the habit
now it's time to take responsibility
for your actions
time to kick the habit

you're on a high
all the time
waiting for the day you die
take this needle
that you feel
from your body till you keel
to the pain
in your veins
reinvigorate your brain
cause it's a long way home

cause it's a long way home
it's a long way home from nowhere.

"HAUNT"

You said "Trav this is over now I'm gonna go"
but what if this nightmare was just for show?
I shouldn't have let you leave me alone
but everything beautiful needs room to grow

what if one of these days falls into tomorrow?
then surely your face will disappear
what if one of these days falls away to tomorrow?
then surely your face will haunt me here

people and places surrounding me
I have nowhere to go stuck in misery
a call to the heavens, a call to be free
I'm leaving behind what was once a part of me
I'm lacking the answers to the questions I have
I'm lost in the sickness of what I once had
this disease overcomes me but I'm safe at last
you left me bleeding but my heart forgets fast

what if one of these days falls into tomorrow?
then surely your face will disappear
what if one of these days falls away to tomorrow?
then surely your face will haunt me here

you said "Trav this is over now I'm gonna go"
but what if this nightmare was just for show?
I shouldn't have let you leave me alone
but everything beautiful needs room to grow

what if one of these days falls into tomorrow?
then surely your face will disappear
what if one of these days falls away to tomorrow?
then surely your face will haunt me here

if this is a nightmare
then when will it end?
I'm tired of dreaming
tired of pretend
if this is a nightmare
then when will it end?
I'm tired of dreaming
tired of pretend

my heart may forget
but I'm still stuck dreaming of you
haunted by you.

"DEATH TO AN ANGEL"

It's my unhappy ending to happy things
it's this terrible nightmare that darkness brings
it's over the rainbow but buried under dirt
it's a photograph finish with stains on your shirt
it's the right to the wrong but nobody cares
it's you lying here naked or in underwear
it's the breaking of a window with glass on the floor
it's putting back the barriers that were there before
it's everything beautiful, it's everything dead
it's everything I want to be, all the stupid things I said
it's staring into nothing with dreams in your eyes
it's that sudden upset stomach when you finally realize
it's feeling so helpless, it's feeling so numb
it's the end of our beginning that never did come
it's my unhappy ending to happy things
it's me broken hearted as you spread your wings
and fly into the sun, please wake me so it can all be undone.

"THE GREAT DIVIDE PART 2: FACELESS"

Looking back can you see our faces?
staring at you but you were faceless
can you see how much this hurt?
even after all these years my eyes still burn

you left us alone with nowhere to hide
from the pain you placed upon our doorstep and swept inside
it doesn't go away, it doesn't get better
I hope it breaks your heart to read this letter
cause today is a lot like yesterday
filling me with dreams that never stay
and today is a lot like yesterday
my broken dreams of you they never stay

looking back can you see our faces?
staring at you but you were faceless
can you see how much this hurt?
even after all these years my eyes still burn

I wake up with no one in my life
every morning I struggle to open my eyes
tears that make me sleep have sealed them shut
though it seems to me this way I'm better off
cause today is just another day
waiting to crush me and brush me away
and today is just another day
I won't let you crush me and brush me away
it's over I'm done with you

looking back can you see our faces?
staring at you but you were faceless
can you see how much this hurt?
even after all these years my eyes still burn

    it's over I'm done with you
    it's over I'm done with you
    we'll never say goodbye
    never again cry
    we'll never say goodbye
    never again cry
    it's over I'm done with you

looking back can you see our faces?
staring at you but you were faceless
can you see how much this hurt?
even after all these years my eyes still burn

    cause you were so faceless.

"MEMORIES REMAIN"

What do you do when the sun won't shine?
cause I'm stuck in this gloom of mine
we used to talk, we used to run together
the last time I saw you I can't even remember
and what do you do when your days are cold?
sleeping with the light on cause you're afraid to be alone
you lost the one who truly guides the way
hanging onto the words you couldn't say

but this heart doesn't forget easily
all the time we spent we felt so free
but I'm trapped, bound and gagged on the floor
like a rat, caged and searching for the door

what do you do when the nights don't end?
the day becomes a faded memory in your head
and darkness seems to be your only hope
insanity will come to help you cope
so what do you do when all that's real is gone?
all that's left is all that went wrong
my remedy lies in this knife and these pills
once and for all I'm going for the kill

and this heart doesn't forget easily
all the time we spent we felt so free
but I'm trapped, bound and gagged on the floor
like a rat, caged and searching for the door

we can't relive the past
but we can try to put the past behind
try to move on with our lives
we can't relive the past
but we can try to put the past behind
try to move on with our lives
well I can't without you

cause this heart doesn't forget easily
all the time we spent we felt so free
but I'm trapped, bound and gagged on the floor
like a rat, caged and searching for the door
this heart doesn't forget easily
all the time we spent we felt so free
but I'm trapped, bound and gagged on the floor
like a rat, caged and searching for the door

we can't relive the past
but I can't move on without you
cause the memories will always remain.

"PORCELAIN"

I didn't see the sun today
cause you keep it hidden, hidden from me
and I watched the world through my eyes turn gray
your porcelain face, porcelain face

it's been a while since I could say that I was fine
I've been in denial pretending everything is alright
it's been a while since I could say that I was fine
I've been in denial pretending everything is alright

I forgot to take my pills today
they keep you hidden, hidden from me
and I lost myself somewhere far away
in your porcelain face, porcelain face

it's been a while since I could say that I was fine
I've been in denial pretending everything is alright
it's been a while since I could say that I was fine
I've been in denial pretending everything is alright

I didn't see the sun today
cause you keep it hidden, hidden from me
and I watched the world through my eyes turn gray
your porcelain face, porcelain face
I forgot to take my pills today
they keep you hidden, hidden from me
and I lost myself somewhere far away
in your porcelain face, porcelain face

it's been a while since I could say that I was fine
I've been in denial pretending everything is alright
it's been a while since I could say that I was fine
I've been in denial pretending everything is alright

I wish I could see your smile
cause it's been a while
your porcelain face, porcelain face
I wish I could see your smile
cause it's been a while
your porcelain face, porcelain face

it's been a while since I could say that I was fine
I've been in denial pretending everything is alright
it's been a while since I could say that I was fine
I've been in denial pretending everything is alright

I've been lost in your porcelain face, porcelain face for a while.

"BREATHLESS"

You
wanted me
to be
everything
and you
wanted me
to see
everything
but I'm
no good
at this
anymore
and I
don't do
what I'm told
this is for
you
and me
but we're
breaking to pieces
of my heart
in your hands
they're falling to the floor
by the bed
where you slept
when you left me breathless
with the
sight of
your beauty
your wonderful beauty
you still leave me breathless with your beauty.

"A PLAGUE INFECTS US ALL"

You walked away the last time today
you left me to bleed with my disease
and you tore apart my fragile heart
it was the only thing that kept me sane
that I held onto when I was without you
I've been living a lie
so now I'm giving up to die

am I the only one that you let down?
with your empty promises watch me hit the ground
are you there for them cause you were never there for me
you were never there, you were never there
you were the only one I looked up to
show me the way just like I wanted you to
don't turn your back when I need you more than before
you were never there, you are never there

you walked away the last time today
you left me to bleed with my disease
and you tore apart my fragile heart
it was the only thing that kept me sane
that I held onto when I was without you
I've been living a lie
so now I'm giving up to die

I've seen your ignorance it ruins lives
pretending not to notice, you're so contrived
I've joined the rest in our fight to spread the word
you are never there, you are never there
stricken slowly we will meet our end
we will suffer more than you can even imagine
but anything's better than dying in your arms or waking to your face
cause you are never there and you will never be there

you walked away the last time today
you left me to bleed with my disease
and you tore apart my fragile heart
it was the only thing that kept me sane
that I held onto when I was without you
I've been living a lie
so now I'm giving up to die

a plague…infects…us all
one by one we're starting to fall
a plague…infects…us all
one by one we're starting to fall
a plague…infects…us all
one by one we're starting to fall
a plague…infects…us all
one by one we're starting to fall

you walked away the last time today
you left me to bleed with my disease
and you tore apart my fragile heart
it was the only thing that kept me sane
that I held onto when I was without you
I've been living a lie
so now I'm giving up to die

you choose the light
I choose my right to
you choose the light
I choose my right to
you choose the light
I choose my right to
you choose the light
I choose my right to decide.

"CRYSTAL BALL"

Did you believe
that this would come to be?
the end of you and me
as far as I can see
the end of you and me

so take a look in your crystal ball
see if you can predict the fall
this time it's not my fault
this time it's not my fault
try again just to see inside
trick yourself into believing lies
this time it's not my fault
this time it's not my fault

are you afraid
of your mistakes?
you pushed me away
you're trying not to break
as far as I can see
the end of you and me

so take a look in your crystal ball
see if you can predict the fall
this time it's not my fault
this time it's not my fault
try again just to see inside
trick yourself into believing lies
this time it's not my fault
this time it's not my fault

you were the only one for me
but I was just another game for you to play
you were the only one for me
but I was just another game for you to play
you were the only one for me
but I was just another game for you to play
you were the only one for me
but I was just another game for you to play

don't you forget
all the time we spent
and I hope you regret
the day we ever met
as far as I can see
you're dead to me

so take a look in your crystal ball
see if you can predict the fall
this time it's not my fault
this time it's not my fault
try again just to see inside
trick yourself into believing lies
this time it's not my fault
this time it's not my fault

so take a look in your crystal ball
so take a look in your crystal ball
so take a look in your crystal ball
and see this is all YOUR FAULT.

"A PART OF ME..."

You said that things would never change
but now you're gone
you said that you couldn't feel the same
where did I go wrong?
you broke my heart, you broke my will
you tore me down
you've given up cause you lost the thrill
so I'm left out

and at the end of the day
you won't be running back to me
cause you have said goodbye for
the last time
and at the end of the day
you won't be running back to me
cause you have said goodbye for
the last time

you said that you would always be
but you just lied
if you open your eyes you'll see
a part of me died
just listen to the words I say
we'll be alright
don't walk, don't run, don't crawl away
you're breaking me inside

and at the end of the day
you won't be running back to me
cause you have said goodbye for
the last time
and at the end of the day
you won't be running back to me
cause you have said goodbye for
the last time

but I still need you
and I still want you
and I still love you
but I still need you
and I still want you
and I still love you

and at the end of the day
you won't be running back to me
cause you have said goodbye for
the last time
and at the end of the day
you won't be running back to me
cause you have said goodbye for
the last time

a part of me cried
a part of me died
a part of me never said goodbye
a part of me cried
a part of me died
a part of me never said goodbye
a part of me…
a part of me…
you were a part of me.

"POISON IN MY MOUTH"

You sit alone and wonder where I am
am I coming home or did you miss your chance?
to say you love me, to show that you care
time keeps winding, you'll end up alone and scared

her kiss that blew me away
you made me realize I had nothing to say
and everything that I gave
was all for nothing cause I threw it all away
for just one kiss

I sit alone but I know why you left
are you coming home so I can fix this mess?
I said I'm sorry, I didn't mean to make you cry
and now I'm lonely without you in my life

her kiss that blew me away
you made me realize I had nothing to say
and everything that I gave
was all for nothing cause I threw it all away
for just one kiss

we sit alone, what else can we do?
we're stuck in love but we can't break through
you won't forgive me for my one mistake
I'll prove I love you for as long as it takes
I'll do whatever it takes

her kiss that blew me away
you made me realize I had nothing to say
and everything that I gave
was all for nothing cause I threw it all away
for just one kiss

this is not how I wanted it to be
I'm so sorry
I'm so sorry
this is not how I wanted it to be
I'm so sorry
I'm so sorry
this is not how I wanted it to be
I'm so sorry
I'm so sorry
this is not how I wanted it to be
I'm so sorry
I'm so sorry

her kiss that blew me away
you made me realize I had nothing to say
and everything that I gave
was all for nothing cause I threw it all away
for just one kiss

there's a cure to this poison in my mouth
but I just can't seem to reach you right now.

"SO TIRED"

Sex is more to me than just a tease
but you lost your appetite to please
and you left me in the cold again
I'm finding reasons now for us to end
love is more to me than mystery
it complicates things so easily
and you only care about yourself
the time has come that I find someone else

I'm so tired of feeling alone
I'm so tired of feeling worthless
and so when all these days have gone
I'll be just a memory
I'm so tired of feeling alone
I'm so tired of feeling worthless
and so when all these days have gone
I'll be just a memory

you tear apart the pieces of my heart
when you tell me you lied from the start
I lose myself when you're not by my side
but something's gotta give to make you try
you take for granted all I've given you
but nothing in return for all I do
a little affection is all I ask
I tried so hard but couldn't make this last

I'm so tired of feeling alone
I'm so tired of feeling worthless
and so when all these days have gone
I'll be just a memory
I'm so tired of feeling alone
I'm so tired of feeling worthless
and so when all these days have gone
I'll be just a memory

I'm so tired
so sick and tired of this
I'm so tired
so sick and tired of this
I'm so tired
so sick and tired of this
I'm so tired
so tired

I'm so tired of feeling alone
I'm so tired of feeling worthless
and so when all these days have gone
I'll be just a memory
I'm so tired of feeling alone
I'm so tired of feeling worthless
and so when all these days have gone
I'll be just a memory

I'll be your reminder of the mistake you made
I'll be just your memory.

"HOME"

I'll take this razor to my wrists
and leave you with nothing
I won't forgive you for all of this
keep my blood gushing
and I won't sleep tonight
cause you put up a fight
another sleepless night alone
won't bring you home

and after the fall
you'll be wishing for one more day
cause I will be gone
your whole life will be in disarray
and after the fall
you'll be wishing for one more day
cause I will be gone
your whole life will tremble and break away

I'll tie this noose around my throat
and tighten the pressure
kick out the chair and just let go
I'll never forget her
and you won't sleep tonight
cause I gave up this fight
another sleepless night alone
won't bring me home

and after the fall
you'll be wishing for one more day
cause I will be gone
your whole life will be in disarray
and after the fall
you'll be wishing for one more day
cause I will be gone
your whole life will tremble and break away

home is where the heart is
but you're watching as my life ends
home is where the heart is
but you're watching as my life ends

and after the fall
you'll be wishing for one more day
cause I will be gone
your whole life will be in disarray
and after the fall
you'll be wishing for one more day
cause I will be gone
your whole life will tremble and break away

COME HOME
COME HOME
COME HOME
before it's too late.

"I MISS YOU"

It used to be that I was never there
then it became you never cared
how does someone just give up love?
I'm begging you to explain this just once
and tell me where does all that love go?
did you feel it or was it just for show?
cause you led me on and on and on
I'll suffocate myself with this song

how could you do this to me?
we were supposed to be
and I want you so badly
I need you, it's so maddening
cause I miss you
oh god I miss you

it used to be you loved me so much
but it seems you've grown out of touch
with emotions you've buried deep inside
I don't understand why you run and hide
how can you walk away after so long?
now I know the meaning of alone
and none of this really seems to fair
I'd give my life just to have you here

how could you do this to me?
we were supposed to be
and I want you so badly
I need you, it's so maddening
cause I miss you
oh god I miss you

I was all you needed before
why isn't that good enough anymore?
I thought we were forever
now we're not even together
I was all you needed before
why isn't that good enough anymore?
I thought we were forever
now we're not even together

how could you do this to me?
we were supposed to be
and I want you so badly
I need you, it's so maddening
cause I miss you
oh god I miss you

I miss you
I miss you.

"TURN THE PAGE"

When I look into your eyes
I get a feeling
that I thought I lost inside
I was bleeding
but you came into my life
now I'm breathing
cause we just seem so right
I'm completed
this pain defeated

never look back at the problems I've had
I've been broken hearted but now I'm starting
to write a new page that won't be the same
I've done this before, I won't fuck it up anymore

when I'm holding you so tight
I get a feeling
from the chemicals in my mind
I was kneeling
in the tears that I have cried
now I'm healing
cause I found you here tonight
I'm completed
this pain defeated

never look back at the problems I've had
I've been broken hearted but now I'm starting
to write a new page that won't be the same
I've done this before, I won't fuck it up anymore

when one door closes another one opens
she left me alone but you gave me a reason
to always smile and keep my head up
I'll turn the page and finally move on

never look back at the problems I've had
I've been broken hearted but now I'm starting
to write a new page that won't be the same
I've done this before, I won't fuck it up anymore

when one door closes another one opens
she left me alone but you gave me a reason
to always smile and keep my head up
I'll turn the page and finally move on

I'll turn the page
turn the page
turn the page and move on
I'll turn the page
turn the page
turn the page and move on
I'm finally moving on.

"IS THIS LOVE?"

I just wanna see you again
I just met you but it feels like I've known you forever
is this where we begin?
I need you to know I've never found anyone better

and I'm uncovering holes
that were left in my soul
but you fill them right up
is this love? is this love? is this love?
is this love? is this love? is this love?

I love your hair and those blue eyes
I love your laugh and how it makes me forget her
and you are my only sunshine
I dream of you and it seems nothing else matters

and I'm uncovering holes
that were left in my soul
but you fill them right up
is this love? is this love? is this love?
is this love? is this love? is this love?

this only comes once in a lifetime
I'm not stopping until I make you mine
cause I've never felt anything like this
I won't let it be the chance that I miss

and I'm uncovering holes
that were left in my soul
but you fill them right up
is this love? is this love? is this love?
is this love? is this love? is this love?

this only comes once in a lifetime
I'm not stopping until I make you mine
cause I've never felt anything like this
I won't let it be the chance that I miss
cause this is love, this is love, this is love
this is love, this is love, this is love.

"ONLY TIME"

I used to think about you everyday
but since I've been without you I'm okay
and now there's nothing left to make me stay
I've waited long enough for you so go away

    cut my emotions like a chainsaw
    watch me bleed you away
    maybe then you'll realize
    why you should have stayed
    give back the innocence you've stolen
    watch me die inside
    cause you left me lying here broken
    alone with only time

I used to dream about you every night
and wake to find you missing every time
so I no longer feel like holding tight
it's over but I know I'll be alright

    cut my emotions like a chainsaw
    watch me bleed you away
    maybe then you'll realize
    why you should have stayed
    give back the innocence you've stolen
    watch me die inside
    cause you left me lying here broken
    alone with only time

I used to beat myself up over you
but you lived a lie that never will be true
and now it's safe to say that we are through
my only mistake was ever loving you

cut my emotions like a chainsaw
watch me bleed you away
maybe then you'll realize
why you should have stayed
give back the innocence you've stolen
watch me die inside
cause you left me lying here broken
alone with only time

angels your demons they won't save you now
pulling the trigger your only way out
angels my demons they won't save me now
pulling the trigger.

"THE ANSWERS YOU FIND WILL KILL YOU"

Come awake in a hospital bed
it will remind you of what you did
how can you always be so selfish?
what could make you always feel so worthless?
you won't be able to forget with these scars
all the times that you slipped too far
and everyone that was by your side
won't stick around just to watch you die

close your eyes
to the questions in your mind
cause the answers that you find
will kill you
close your eyes
to the questions in your mind
cause the answers that you find
will kill you

come awake on the bathroom floor
this seems eerily familiar to before
how did you let things get this bad?
what could possibly make you feel so sad?
cause every time you stand you fall again
making you think that this time it's the end
you won't be able to leave these thoughts behind
you're finding release in this suicide

close your eyes
to the questions in your mind
cause the answers that you find
will kill you
close your eyes
to the questions in your mind
cause the answers that you find
will kill you

you try so hard to make it out alive
but you're torn apart by the answers you find
you try so hard to make it out alive
but you're torn apart by the answers you find
you try so hard to make it out alive
but you're torn apart by the answers you find
you try so hard to make it out alive
but you're torn apart by the answers you find

close your eyes
to the questions in your mind
cause the answers that you find
will kill you
close your eyes
to the questions in your mind
cause the answers that you find
will kill you
will kill you

they've killed you, you're gone.

"THE SOUND OF SILENCE"

Somebody talk to me
and tell me everything is alright
I just can't take that step ahead
I'm scared I'll trip and fall behind
and everything I know
is crashing to these streets I'm walking on
the silence suffocates the sound
of my broken hearted song
and all this thinking sends a shiver
paralyze my spinal cord
so what's the use in loving deeply
when the chemicals distort?
and everything inside my brain
is screaming bloody blasphemy
the silence suffocates the sound
of my last guilt stricken plea

I won't make it, I won't make it, I won't make it on my own
I can't take it, I can't take it, I can't take this anymore
I am jaded, I am jaded, I am jaded and alone
I am fading, I am fading, I am fading into oblivion

somebody talk to me
and tell me everything will be okay
I feel the pressure building
I just want to try to walk away
but every time I take a step
it sets me two steps back
the feeling's getting stronger
I'm not sure I can sustain this attack
and all this poison in my body
I'm convulsing violently
so what's the point in even living
when my apologies just bleed?
onto the floor of this here room
where I lay shattered, motionless
the silence suffocates the sound
of me gasping my last breath

I won't make it, I won't make it, I won't make it on my own
I can't take it, I can't take it, I can't take this anymore
I am jaded, I am jaded, I am jaded and alone
I am fading, I am fading, I am fading into oblivion

nobody talked to me to tell me everything was just fine
now it's too late and you'll be horrified by what you will find
all that remains of my depleted, hopeless, helpless life
is what you just shrugged off and cast away and left here to die
nobody talked to me to tell me everything was just fine
now it's too late and you'll be horrified by what you will find
all that remains of my depleted, hopeless, helpless life
is what you just shrugged off and cast away and left here to die

I won't make it, I won't make it, I won't make it on my own
I can't take it, I can't take it, I can't take this anymore
I am jaded, I am jaded, I am jaded and alone
I am fading, I am fading, I am fading into oblivion

I didn't make it, didn't make it, didn't make it on my own
I couldn't take it, couldn't take it, couldn't take this anymore
I was jaded, I was jaded, I was jaded and alone
now I've faded, now I've faded, now I've faded into oblivion

and you didn't hear a word of it at all.

"STARLIT SKY"

You make me feel like I have never felt before
all your time spent here still I'm left begging for more
you came, you saw, you went away
my heart you stole, I'll soon decay
you make me feel like I am floating on air
one day you'll see that we are the perfect pair
you look so sweet, you are divine
my heart is yours, say yours is mine

if I could make you love me
I would give you the world
I'd show you possibility
your heart is my pearl
if I could make you love me
I would open your eyes
to a brand new point of view of me
you're my starlit midnight sky

you make me feel like I am truly alive
with you here with me there is no mountain I can't climb
you give, you take, my only hope
my heart is yours, don't let this go
you make me feel like I can smile again
say when you come home we'll be more than just friends
your hair, your eyes, a miracle
my heart you stole, you're beautiful

if I could make you love me
I would give you the world
I'd show you possibility
your heart is my pearl
if I could make you love me
I would open your eyes
to a brand new point of view of me
you're my starlit midnight sky

my sky has never been so empty
since you left me
my sky has never been so empty
since you left me
my sky has never been so empty
since you left me
I wish I could tell you this

if I could make you love me
I would give you the world
I'd show you possibility
your heart is my pearl
if I could make you love me
I would open your eyes
to a brand new point of view of me
you're my starlit midnight sky

everything I do from this point on
everything's for you till you're in my arms.

"ACROSS THE WORLD"

You're on a plane
flying back to your boyfriend
as I write this song for you
but I'll be okay
cause this is just the beginning
I struck the match that burns for you
I'll torch this city
and illuminate the sky
as I sit and think of you
it'll look so pretty
your silhouette in the moonlight
still nothing quite compares to you

so next time we stand face to face again
all my words will come out right
and if not I'll just sing this song to you
so you will know exactly what I'm feeling inside
we could run away forever
we could finally be together
and everything will be alright

you're on a plane
flying across the world
how'd I let this pass me by?
I'm not okay
cause you're the perfect girl
I've been waiting for my whole life
I'll drown in my dreams
and wake in a cold sweat
cause it's you that's swimming in my mind
without you near me
I'm almost better off dead
but to see you again I know I must survive

so next time we stand face to face again
all my words will come out right
and if not I'll just sing this song to you
so you will know exactly what I'm feeling inside
we could run away forever
we could finally be together
and everything will be alright

you're keeping me alive
just the thought of you could make me or break me
I don't want to die
I need to fix all the mistakes I've been making
you're keeping me alive
just the thought of you could make me or break me
I don't want to die
I need to fix all the mistakes I've been making
I need the chance to let you know

so next time we stand face to face again
all my words will come out right
and if not I'll just sing this song to you
so you will know exactly what I'm feeling inside
we could run away forever
we could finally be together
and everything will be alright

and I would be alright
if I could just let you know.

"BREAKING UP IS THE FIRST STEP TOWARDS RECOVERY"

You watched me fall
sinking deeper than either of us thought
and I'm such a mess
it's plain to see you were my last line of defense
you let me go this time
forever was a lie
you cut me down
scars and bruises are what define me now
I've come so far
I've left behind the broken fragments of my heart
you let me go this time
forever just wasn't right

I'll never forgive you for what you have done
I'm mending all the pieces and I'm back to where I started from
you almost killed me with this devastating blow
as far as I'm concerned you're dead to me and I'll let go
I'll never forgive you for what you have done
I'm mending all the pieces and I'm back to where I started from
you almost killed me with this devastating blow
as far as I'm concerned you're dead to me and I'll let go

you watched me slide
shadows hid from you the tears in my eyes
and I'm moving on
we dragged this out and tortured ourselves for too long
you let me go this time
forever became benign
you were so fake
it seems you're becoming my least favorite mistake
I'm better off
since you've been gone I'm starting to feel like myself
you let me go this time
forever has changed my life

I'll never forgive you for what you have done
I'm mending all the pieces and I'm back to where I started from
you almost killed me with this devastating blow
as far as I'm concerned you're dead to me and I'll let go
I'll never forgive you for what you have done
I'm mending all the pieces and I'm back to where I started from
you almost killed me with this devastating blow
as far as I'm concerned you're dead to me and I'll let go

you won't see me in the waiting room
it's only for family and friends
you won't be there in the waiting room
it's only for family and friends
today my life begins
today my life begins again

I'll never forgive you for what you have done
I'm mending all the pieces and I'm back to where I started from
you almost killed me with this devastating blow
as far as I'm concerned you're dead to me and I'll let go
I'll never forgive you for what you have done
I'm mending all the pieces and I'm back to where I started from
you almost killed me with this devastating blow
as far as I'm concerned you're dead to me and I'll let go

the halo I saw above your head
it came crashing on me instead.

"FAILED APOLOGIES"

I wanna sit right down and talk to you
you can tell me everything you always wanted to
I wanna sit right down and share with you
all the pain I feel inside, what I've been through

but your failed apologies are deafening
you are the mess I made of everything
I'll never forgive you for all of this
I'll finally forget you once I slit my wrists
and bleed myself
free of you

I wanna sit right down and SCREAM AT YOU
tell you how much I hate all the things you do
I wanna sit right down and laugh at you
all the lies you told, well guess what? I lied too

but your failed apologies are deafening
you are the mess I made of everything
I'll never forgive you for all of this
I'll finally forget you once I slit my wrists
and bleed myself
free of you

I don't wanna sit here with you anymore
waiting for the day that I can even the score
I don't wanna sit here with you anymore
today I'm gonna settle the score
I'm moving on tonight
to the afterlife

but your failed apologies are deafening
you are the mess I made of everything
I'll never forgive you for all of this
I'll finally forget you once I slit my wrists
and bleed myself
free of you
your failed apologies are deafening
you are the mess I made of everything
I'll never forgive you for all of this
I'll finally forget you once I slit my wrists
and bleed myself
free of you

my blood will stain your hands forever…forever…forever.

"TIME TO LET GO"

I saw my life dance at my fingertips
just out of reach I can't grab hold of it
you used to be something so close to me
now you've become the object of my misery
I'm left here drowning in a lonesome hate
but how long can I keep up this charade?
cause secrets buried say I still love you
no one will know but me, I hide the truth

years go by and I wonder why
you are still here on my mind
the days are long and the months are slow
I think it's time I just let go
but it's easier said than done
when I thought you were the one
there's nothing left of me to show
I think it's time I just let go

time became our biggest enemy
it teased us with the thought that we could be
then ripped my heart out when you just gave up
I never thought I'd hear you say you're not in love
the silence has become unbearable
tearing at my mind till I can't be consoled
and I'm a mess of what I used to be
nothing remains that remotely resembles me

years go by and I wonder why
you are still here on my mind
the days are long and the months are slow
I think it's time I just let go
but it's easier said than done
when I thought you were the one
there's nothing left of me to show
I think it's time I just let go

take what I have to offer
even though it isn't much
try to make this last forever
even though you've had enough
give me a chance to make this better
after all our shitty luck
I won't say this forever
I tried, I failed, my love

years go by and I wonder why
you are still here on my mind
the days are long and the months are slow
I think it's time I just let go
but it's easier said than done
when I thought you were the one
there's nothing left of me to show
I think it's time I just let go

just know that wherever I go you'll be
and wherever you go I'll see
cause we're under the same sky
tonight and for the rest of our lives.

"FOOL FOR YOU"

Why do you play tricks on me?
don't you see I'm broken so easily?
why do you fuck with my heart?
don't you see you're more than just a one time scar?
when did your love fade away?
was it when you found that I've made mistakes?
when did your heart let me go?
I've been torn to shreds by all the lies you told

    fool me once
    shame on me
    fool me twice
    shame on you
    but you've fooled me three times
    cause I'm still just a fool for you

where did you go when you left?
was he all the expectations I never met?
and where do we go from here?
this cut gets deeper whenever you are near
what will it take to get you back?
I've bled before but I've never bled like that
what did it mean when you cried?
you were the one who left and I'm the one who died

    fool me once
    shame on me
    fool me twice
    shame on you
    but you've fooled me three times
    cause I'm still just a fool for you

this noose around my neck
this knife across my wrists
this bullet in my head
you are the cause of this
this noose around my neck
this knife across my wrists
this bullet in my head
you are the cause of this
now you can live with what you did

fool me once
shame on me
fool me twice
shame on you
but you've fooled me three times
cause I'm still just a fool for you
fool me once
shame on me
fool me twice
shame on you
but you've fooled me three times
cause I'm still just a fool for you

now can you live with what you did?

"TEAR SHED ROSES"

Why do you pull me down?
I'm like a tree that's been burnt to the ground
and why do you play these games?
I've been hurt before but never quite this way
my heart is broken again
you took my life and tore it from end to end
and now I'm cringing inside
cause I lost the only thing that kept me alive

love is flowing through my veins
and spilling out my pores
all the times you've gone away
still I keep coming back for more
and when it's all said and done
you know I'll be the one
that keeps on running back to you

why do you fuck with me?
I'm like a tidal wave that's lost out at sea
and why are you so screwed up?
breaking me once was just never enough
now I'm begging for you
to just let me go if what you're saying is true
or tell me otherwise
cause I can't take this endless drowning in your eyes

love is flowing through my veins
and spilling out my pores
all the times you've gone away
still I keep coming back for more
and when it's all said and done
you know I'll be the one
that keeps on running back to you

you keep me around for your amusement
until I come to my self conclusion
to end this silence, to end this war
I'll give myself and you'll have your cure
and when I die you'll bury me
tear shed roses from your heart's misery
cause you thought you had all this time
but time was never on my side
and now you sit there all alone
wondering how you became so cold
just remember how you took my life
as the blade cuts in and the darkness takes over the light

love is flowing through my veins
and spilling out my pores
all the times you've gone away
still I keep coming back for more
and when it's all said and done
you know I'll be the one
that keeps on running back to you

that keeps on loving you.

"HOW BITTER SWEET IS"

You can sleep with every guy in the world
cause that's what sluts like you do
but you'll never forget my kiss
you'll never forget my touch
you'll never forget my fuck
and you'll definitely never forget my love
and when you're alone
no, let me rephrase that
you won't be alone
cause you'll fill the void with another meaningless affection
but when you're old and unhappy and unloved
that's when you'll want me
that's when you'll miss me
that's when you'll love me completely
but it will be too late
and that's when I'll have my revenge
cause that's when your heart will be broken like mine.

"DEAR SEPTEMBER"

You stare at pictures hanging on your wall
you leave them there so you don't forget how things were before
when you were happy and in love
when I was the one that you were dreaming of
you wake up soaking, wondering how things got this way
even though you left you still miss me everyday
cause you were happy and in love
I'll always be the one that you are dreaming of

dear September
your days left me in pieces
I hope you remember
the nights are cold when you're all alone
dear September
your days left me in shambles
I hope you remember
the nights are dark with a broken heart

I stare at pictures sitting on my desk
I put them away so I can stop this aching in my chest
cause I was happy and in love
but something tells me that could never be enough
I wake up shivering cause the bed beside me is cold
it's where you slept and it's the last time I remember being whole
I was happy and in love
but now I'm shaking from the damage you have done

dear September
your days left me in pieces
I hope you remember
the nights are cold when you're all alone
dear September
your days left me in shambles
I hope you remember
the nights are dark with a broken heart

you pick me up just to knock me down
but I will always go another round
you're coming back but it isn't true
this time I know that we are through
when nothing's real and nothing's right
I'll end the hurt with this here knife
your world will shatter like it did before
cause you can't have me anymore
and all that's left are the tears you cry
I'll wait in heaven for the day you die
don't be so sad, I did this for you
not for the pain but the love that we grew

dear September
your days left me in pieces
I hope you remember
the nights are cold when you're all alone
dear September
your days left me in shambles
I hope you remember
the nights are dark with a broken heart.

"ONCE AND FOR ALL (WAKE UP)"

I'll take these broken wings and try to fly away
I'll take these broken dreams and try to make some sense of this
I'll take this broken heart and sew it back together
I'll take this broken life and pick myself up again
tonight I'm gonna take this and make this real
tonight I'm gonna end all the pain I feel
once and for all

once was never quite enough to say what's on my mind
the saddest ending to this story, now it's time to say goodbye
a tragic loss of innocence on this dark, cold night
the saddest ending to this sad story, my last goodbye

I'll take these broken words and throw them in your face
I'll take these broken lies and try to find some truth
I'll take this broken soul and bury it inside
I'll take this broken knife and cut into my wrists again
tonight I'm gonna take this and make this real
tonight I'm gonna end all the pain I feel
once and for all

once was never quite enough to say what's on my mind
the saddest ending to this story, now it's time to say goodbye
a tragic loss of innocence on this dark, cold night
the saddest ending to this sad story, my last goodbye

I'll take these broken chords and play my final note
I'll take these broken rhymes and sing until I'm gone
I'll take this broken hand and write you one last time
I'll take this broken song and send it in a letter to you again
tonight I'm gonna take this and make this real
tonight I'm gonna end all the pain I feel
once and for all

once was never quite enough to say what's on my mind
the saddest ending to this story, now it's time to say goodbye
a tragic loss of innocence on this dark, cold night
the saddest ending to this sad story, my last goodbye

I won't wake up in my own blood
from what I've done
can anyone save me now?
I won't wake up in my own blood
from what I've done
nothing can save me now

once was never quite enough to say what's on my mind
the saddest ending to this story, now it's time to say goodbye
a tragic loss of innocence on this dark, cold night
the saddest ending to this sad story, my last goodbye

I won't, I won't, I won't, I won't wake up
I won't, I won't, I won't WAKE UP.

"SAY HELLO TO LONELINESS"

I'm fighting an endless battle
with the walls that surround me
I'm longing to find within myself
a single moment of clarity
I need an antidote to cure my pain
but I don't know if one exists
so I struggle with these demons
that continue to bind me to loneliness

and it feels like it's all in my head
and it feels like my world's caving in
and it feels like I'm my own best friend
and it feels like I'm becoming me again

I feel all the pressures of the world
resting squarely on my shoulders
to be the man you have to beat the man
but I haven't been the same since I lost her
time spent searching on my own
has left me nothing but displaced
I throw away my everything
and wind up face to face
with loneliness again

and it feels like it's all in my head
and it feels like my world's caving in
and it feels like I'm my own best friend
and it feels like I'm becoming me again

I find sorrow comforting
cause misery loves company
and all the lies I told myself
became another excuse to bleed
and when it all came crashing down
it took my breath away
but when you see me standing here
you'll be the one in disarray
as loneliness invites you in

and it feels like it's all in my head
and it feels like my world's caving in
and it feels like I'm my own best friend
and it feels like I'm becoming me again

you thought I would crumble
when I stumbled and fell
but I can see through this dark
my heart is getting well
you thought I would crumble
when I stumbled and fell
but I can see through this dark
my heart is getting well
and I'll be better than before
so say hello to loneliness you whore.

"SUNSETS LIKE RAINDROPS"

I watched the sun set on the ocean
colors so vibrant, red, purple and blue
and it's said the truth about devotion
is found in a place where I am standing next to you
but the answers that I find bring emptiness
I am left to fight this battle alone
and all I really need is happiness
but I've lost my way and I'm shivering from the cold

rain falls like tears on a summer day
when the rain falls, I wish it would wash this pain away
rain falls like tears on a winter night
when the rain falls, as long as you're here with me I'll be alright

I watched the sun set on the hillside
colors so brilliant, yellow, orange and gray
and it's said the truth about this life
is found in a place where all my fears just fade away
but the questions that I have are surfacing
I am left to fight this war alone
and all I need is you to call my name
so I can finally find my way back home

rain falls like tears on a summer day
when the rain falls, I wish it would wash this pain away
rain falls like tears on a winter night
when the rain falls, as long as you're here with me I'll be alright

I watched the sun set on the mountain top
colors so extravagant you'd think it was a dream
and it's said the truth about true love
is found in a place where I'm the only one you need
but the fact remains there's more than meets the eye
I am left to tread this path alone
until the day you're standing by my side
cause in my heart and in my mind, you're the only one I know

rain falls like tears on a summer day
when the rain falls, I wish it would wash this pain away
rain falls like tears on a winter night
when the rain falls, as long as you're here with me I'll be alright

no despair
when I find you there
love is in the air
no one else can compare
no despair
when I find you here
love is in the air
no one else can compare

rain falls like tears on a summer day
when the rain falls, I wish it would wash this pain away
rain falls like tears on a winter night
when the rain falls, as long as you're here with me I'll be alright.

"THE HUNGER, THE RAPTURE, THE TOAST"

Temptation rears it's ugly head in times of broken trust
it takes a hold of everything with intentions to crush
and madness takes control of what we thought was in our grasp
tonight we toast to feelings that got lost in the past

and the hunger
it grows within
and the hunger
it gets larger with sin
and the hunger
it'll spread to your skin
and the hunger
it will always win

temptation rears it's ugly head in times of broken love
it seizes every moment that we built from the ground up
and sanity is questioned when we throw it all away
tonight we toast to the future and the life we couldn't maintain

and the hunger
it grows within
and the hunger
it gets larger with sin
and the hunger
it'll spread to your skin
and the hunger
it will always win

temptation rears it's ugly head in times of broken truth
as lies get burned within our hearts until we are consumed
and reality is haunting as we share our final kiss
tonight we toast to honesty and the shattered dreams we promised

and the hunger
it grows within
and the hunger
it gets larger with sin
and the hunger
it'll spread to your skin
and the hunger
it will always win

we were caught in the rapture for oh so long
we were caught in the rapture but now it's gone
we were caught in the rapture for oh so long
we were caught in the rapture but now it's gone
I've moved on to someone new
someone who's better than you

and the hunger
it grows within
and the hunger
it gets larger with sin
and the hunger
it'll spread to your skin
and the hunger
it will always win
and the hunger
it grows within
and the hunger
it gets larger with sin
and the hunger
it'll spread to your skin
and the hunger
it will always win.

"A RIVER RED"

Wallowing in self destruction
contemplating suicide
somewhere far she's lost forever
she'll never see the changing tide
she's given up on life too early
she didn't think she had a choice
she's caught up in her own confusion
she had to put an end to all the noise

falling away from everything
never knowing where to begin
crashing down to a bitter end
never knowing what it's like to live
missing out on the chance to live
from beginning to end

staring at his own reflection
conjuring his alibi
the note it reads "I'm gone forever"
his family will surely cry
he's given up on life this evening
he didn't see another way out
he closed his eyes and started drifting
he knew it was too late to turn back now

falling away from everything
never knowing where to begin
crashing down to a bitter end
never knowing what it's like to live
missing out on the chance to live
from beginning to end

watching as their lives are fading
down the drain a river red
they tried to stop the pain from aching
but pain is all they found instead
watching as my life is dripping
down the drain a river red
I tried to stop this constant itching
but my only escape is dead

falling away from everything
never knowing where to begin
crashing down to a bitter end
never knowing what it's like to live
missing out on the chance to live
from beginning to end

see yourself in someone else to try to find the answer
but what you see is make believe and you have no more chances.

"BLANKET OF NOTHING"

My smile hides
the truth inside of my heart
this lonely road
leads us to miles apart
my face disguised
the fear is overwhelming
this road I'm on
keeps me from ever knowing

when you said you loved me
I believed every word
and when you said you're leaving
I couldn't believe what I had heard
and when you came back again
my heart it felt alive
and when you left me again
I almost died
but I won't let you get the best of me this time

my eyes they hide
the demons confined in my head
this solitude
is slowly breaking the skin
the compromise
is more than I could ever take
this loss of blood
is just another cut I've made

when you said you loved me
I believed every word
and when you said you're leaving
I couldn't believe what I had heard
and when you came back again
my heart it felt alive
and when you left me again
I almost died
but I won't let you get the best of me this time

I know I won't find a cure
to the pain that you caused
but I'm willing to fake it
so you can't tell that I'm lost
and as this blanket of nothing
quickly covers my life
I hope you don't try to find me
I hope you don't realize
that the pain that you're feeling
yeah I've felt that pain too
and when you're longing for someone
remember when I held you
your whole body will stiffen
silence pierces to the nerve
and you will finally have nothing
finally get what you deserve

when you said you loved me
I believed every word
and when you said you're leaving
I couldn't believe what I had heard
and when you came back again
my heart it felt alive
and when you left me again
I almost died
but I won't let you get the best of me this time

no I won't let you get the best of me this time.

"WHAT ONCE WAS PURE NOW IS TAINTED"

I'm still hopelessly in love with you
but I'm trying not to show it
and even though you loved me too
still somehow we're broken
and all the pieces of our life
they wound up in your hands
don't let them fall, don't let them die
cause tonight is our last chance

everything beautiful dies sometimes
when everything pure is tainted
and everything wonderful to your surprise
will leave you alone and jaded
but we don't have to be like that

you're still hopelessly in love with me
but you refuse to admit it
despite how hard I try to make you see
still you pretend to feel different
and all the pieces of the last 4 years
are dangling from your fingers
don't let them fall like these desperate tears
cause tonight can make all the difference

everything beautiful dies sometimes
when everything pure is tainted
and everything wonderful to your surprise
will leave you alone and jaded
but we don't have to be like that

you took everything away from me
when you left me behind
you took everything away from me
now I'm starting to realize
you took everything away from me
when you left me behind
you took everything away from me
now I'm starting to find
you'll be the one who misses me
you'll be the one who cries
you'll be the one who's coming back to me
I'll be the one who denies

everything beautiful dies sometimes
when everything pure is tainted
and everything wonderful to your surprise
will leave you alone and jaded
but we don't have to be like that

you stabbed me in the back
so now it has to be like that
you promised forever
forever seems so long ago.

"THROWING BRICKS IN GLASS HOUSES (BREAK OUT)"

We only give what we get back
unless you're stupid old me
I'll give you everything you ask
but I don't get anything I need
cause once again I played the fool
in this game of love and life
what a surprise, this time I lose
but you'll come crashing to your own demise

take this brick and smash it through the window
that's enclosing me tonight
break free of all the pain and sorrow
that's been holding me so tight
take the glass and carve into this body
that's caged me in this skin
break free of all the pain inside me
that's brought me back to bleeding again

I always gave and never received
an endless trend you started yourself
but I won't let your cries deceive
I've got something for your bookshelf
take this, read it and let it consume
cause it's the closest you'll get to me
once, twice, three times I've been used
remember me when you're down on your knees

take this brick and smash it through the window
that's enclosing me tonight
break free of all the pain and sorrow
that's been holding me so tight
take the glass and carve into this body
that's caged me in this skin
break free of all the pain inside me
that's brought me back to bleeding again

I've bled for you
I've bled for me too
I'm dead to you
now I'm dead to me too
I've bled for you
I've bled for me too
I'm dead to you
now I'm dead to me too

take this brick and smash it through the window
that's enclosing me tonight
break free of all the pain and sorrow
that's been holding me so tight
take the glass and carve into this body
that's caged me in this skin
break free of all the pain inside me
that's brought me back to bleeding again

I'll break out as you break down
I'm dying while you're crying
just know that you're the last thing on my mind
before I die.

"HEAVEN'S CALLING"

Haven't you heard yet?
I've been bleeding for a while
nothing can save me
no nothing can save me now
so don't hold your breath
cause you'll be waiting for quite some time
nothing can save you
I'm the only one who can save you now

we both know
how this is gonna go
so save us the trouble and slit your throat
cause we both know
how I let this go
so I'll save us the trouble and tie the rope
around my heart
till I lay lifeless in the dark
and everything we wanted falls apart

when did you hear it?
when did your heart finally break in two?
nothing could save you
but I tried to save you now
I was holding my breath
cause I didn't want to die for you
but nothing could save me
no nothing could save me anyhow

we both know
how this is gonna go
so save us the trouble and slit your throat
cause we both know
how I let this go
so I'll save us the trouble and tie the rope
around my heart
till I lay lifeless in the dark
and everything we wanted falls apart

we could have made it with a little concentration
we could have avoided this mangled devastation
we could have made it with a little more devotion
we could have changed all this negative emotion
we could have made it with a little concentration
we could have avoided this mangled devastation
we could have made it with a little more devotion
we could have changed all this negative emotion
but we ended up lying here
now heaven's calling out to us dear

we both know
how this is gonna go
so save us the trouble and slit your throat
cause we both know
how I let this go
so I'll save us the trouble and tie the rope
around my heart
till I lay lifeless in the dark
and everything we wanted falls apart

you shouldn't have died for me when I died for you
cause what good would that do
you shouldn't have died for me when I died for you
cause what good does that do
but I'll see you again soon
I'll see you when it's through
cause heaven's calling out to me and you.

"PHONE LINE TO YOUR HEART"

You always wanted me to write you a song
well here it is I hope you like it
but I don't know if I can ever be that strong
cause I don't have the strength to fight it
all the while you've held my heart in your hands
even though the years have passed us by
and I'd do anything just to hear your voice again
though I still remember it after all this time

it's been so long
since I've seen your face
but I'm holding on
waiting for the day
that you're in my arms
that you're here to stay
but it's been so long
do you remember my name?

Amanda sat there crying undecidedly
we were so young but we were in love
and we knew that we could never be
Amanda listened as the dial tone stopped
we should've stayed but we were afraid
now this phone call's all that we've got

it's been so long
since I've seen your face
but I'm holding on
waiting for the day
that you're in my arms
that you're here to stay
but it's been so long
do you remember my name?

stop this
silence
I miss
your lips
talking
to me
flows right
through me
I'll take
your wish
best love
best kiss
we tried
leaving
stopped our
hearts beating

it's been so long
since I've seen your face
but I'm holding on
waiting for the day
that you're in my arms
that you're here to stay
but it's been so long
do you remember my name?

Amanda sat there crying undecidedly
we were so young but we were in love
and we knew that we could never be
Amanda listened as the dial tone stopped
we should've stayed but we were afraid
now this phone call's all that we've got

Amanda listen, make the dial tone start
let this phone line lead you back to my heart
cause this phone line leads you back into my heart
leads me back into your heart
leads love back into our hearts.

"LIGHTS AND SIRENS"

What are you afraid of?
death is just a part of this life

can't get you
out of my mind
the last thing these
glazed over eyes
looked upon was
you in his arms
now I'm drowning
water invades my lungs

what are you afraid of?
death is just a part of this life
I am dead
I am dead
I am dead

all that's left are
lights and sirens
taking me to a
place I've never been
where'd I go wrong?
we were so perfect
did I make you
miserable and sick?

what are you afraid of?
death is just a part of this life
I am dead
I am dead
I am dead

part of me died
did you even cry?
you killed me that night
part of me is alive
ambulance that came
medicine in veins
sustaining my brain
to numb and kill the pain

what are you afraid of?
death is just a part of this life
I am dead
I am dead
I am dead

pain is good
it keeps me alive
my purpose for being and feeling survived
and I'm not dead yet

I'M NOT DEAD
I'M NOT DEAD
I'M NOT DEAD

pain is good
it keeps me alive
my purpose for being and feeling survived
and I'm not dead yet.

"RESCUE YOU"

You're enclosed
these four walls in your head
aren't getting any weaker
but you are
you're a mess
this place you call your home
now only serves as shelter
there's no love
you hold on
cause hope is in the distance
but you'll never be strong enough
to pull through

spin, spin, spin around
until you hit the ground
cause what you're looking for is something that can never be found
fall, fall, fall tonight
cause you're losing your mind
when you spill your blood you'll finally know the meaning of life

you're enraged
you blame yourself for everything
but you're just the victim
in this war
you're a wreck
as you lie there on the floor
that's cold and stale like your heart's become
from this hell
you'll give up
think this is not worth living for
try to end this constant torment
in your soul

spin, spin, spin around
until you hit the ground
cause what you're looking for is something that can never be found
fall, fall, fall tonight
cause you're losing your mind
when you spill your blood you'll finally know the meaning of life

take this medication
hurry, quickly drink it up
but it will be too late
this time you are running out of luck
take this medication
hurry, quickly drink it up
but it will be too late
this time you are running out of luck
try to medicate
it will be too late
drink, drink, drink it up
you're running out of luck
and now your time is up

spin, spin, spin around
until you hit the ground
cause what you're looking for is something that can never be found
fall, fall, fall tonight
cause you're losing your mind
when you spill your blood you'll finally know the meaning of life

whisper your last words to no one
wish that they were heard by someone
whisper your last words to no one
wish that they were heard by someone
who could rescue you
who could rescue you.

"A DANCE WITH THE DEVIL CAN ONLY LEAVE YOU DEAD"

This life
this love
was just a game to you
and this heart
of mine
has been broken down for you
over and over again
that house
that street
it still means the same to me
and our sad
goodbye
is the knife that makes me bleed
over and over again
but this time I win

nothing can save you now
when the beat of your heart's on the ground
and when the silence comes rushing in
your mind will be filled with your sins
nothing can save you now
when the demons are crawling out
and when the devil's got you by the hand
you know you're nearing the end

this life
this love
reminds you of what you had
and this heart
of yours
never ever hurt this bad
over and over again
that house
that street
are the reasons that you bleed
our last
goodbye
leaves a scar from a cut too deep
over and over again
cause this time I win

nothing can save you now
when the beat of your heart's on the ground
and when the silence comes rushing in
your mind will be filled with your sins
nothing can save you now
when the demons are crawling out
and when the devil's got you by the hand
you know you're nearing the end

this rope
your throat
equals one last good time
or this blade
your wrist
equals one last good cry
this gun
your head
equals one last red mess
or this pill
your bed
equals a chance I'll never miss
and this time I win

nothing can save you now
when the beat of your heart's on the ground
and when the silence comes rushing in
your mind will be filled with your sins
nothing can save you now
when the demons are crawling out
and when the devil's got you by the hand
you know you're nearing the end

death is now within sight
as the devil takes you home with him tonight.

"CIGARETTE STREET LIGHTS"

Her cigarette is burning
and she found what she's searching for
as she's watching me drown
in a sea of make believe
where nothing's ever what it seems to be
and I can't claw my way out
her hands are shaking
and she found what she's waiting for
but I'm slipping from her grip
into a sea of discontent
cause every word she said she never meant
I'll escape her lying lips

I'm falling for a break down
I'm letting go of everything I've found
I'm running from the pain now
I'm finding there is beauty in my doubt
I'm falling for a break down

my cigarette is ashes
and I found that I wanted more
as I watched her disappear
into a cloud of smoke so thick
where everything I once had makes me sick
and I have never been this scared
but my hands stopped shaking
and I found what's making me cold
as I step out of the dark
into a ray of shining light
where all the past is blinded out of sight
I survived her evil heart

I'm falling for a break down
I'm letting go of everything I've found
I'm running from the pain now
I'm finding there is beauty in my doubt
I'm falling for a break down

these cigarettes lead me away from her
light up the night, carry me from hurt
these cigarettes lead me away from her
light up the night, carry me from hurt
I'm in love with not being in love with you
I'm in love with not being in love with you

anymore

I'm falling for a break down
I'm letting go of everything I've found
I'm running from the pain now
I'm finding there is beauty in my doubt
I'm falling for a break down

I'll use this knife to cut my throat
I'll bleed all the words I never spoke
but don't think I would ever give myself for you again.

"YOU IN THE GROUND MAKES PERFECT SENSE"

This is just another love song
that's gone terribly wrong
I've been writing this for days
but it still always ends up the same
I try to make it sound right
but you're the only thing on my mind
so I'll let emotions take control
and this time it's you I'm aiming for

tonight I'll sneak in through the window and I won't make a sound
make sure that everyone is sleeping and just tip toe around
I'll find my way back to your bedroom where you're lying impaired
I'll take you to my house and in my yard I'll bury you there
I'll never have to hear your voice or see your fucking face
or miss the girl I used to love or the slut that you became

I try so hard not to think of you
but your face is on everything I do
I use this pen to try to let you go
but your name is written in every syllable
don't think this means I'm still in love
I wish I could say I agreed with the above
but these months have shown me you're a fake
and this time it's you whose life's at stake

tonight I'll sneak in through the window and I won't make a sound
make sure that everyone is sleeping and just tip toe around
I'll find my way back to your bedroom where you're lying impaired
I'll take you to my house and in my yard I'll bury you there
I'll never have to hear your voice or see your fucking face
or miss the girl I used to love or the slut that you became

there's only one way for the pain to end
not having you back but having you dead
there's just something about that smile
that makes me want to kill you and not reconcile
there's only one way for the pain to end
not having you back but having you dead
there's just something about that smile
that makes me want to kill you and not reconcile
you're just a lying bitch
I'll never get over it
start saving your strength now
you'll need it to try to dig your way out

tonight I'll sneak in through the window and I won't make a sound
make sure that everyone is sleeping and just tip toe around
I'll find my way back to your bedroom where you're lying impaired
I'll take you to my house and in my yard I'll bury you there
I'll never have to hear your voice or see your fucking face
or miss the girl I used to love or the slut that you became

tonight I won't say goodbye
let the worms do the talking as they're eating you inside.

"IF ONLY I COULD WISH YOU AWAY"

I'll take you by the hand
try to make you understand
I'll take you to a place
where you'll have plenty of space
I'll draw you a picture
or write a new chapter to our adventure

no matter how hard I try
no matter how many days go by
no matter how hard I cry
no matter how many lonely nights
I can't get you off my mind
even after all this time
I still long for the girl I now hate
if only I could wish you away

I'll show you everything
give you what you're missing
I'll make you feel alive
the way you did on those nights
I'll break it down for you
intoxication's all that's gotten me through

no matter how hard I try
no matter how many days go by
no matter how hard I cry
no matter how many lonely nights
I can't get you off my mind
even after all this time
I still long for the girl I now hate
if only I could wish you away

I'll change myself again
forget the nasty things I said
I'll show you true love
the kind we shared for so long
I've been sitting right here
a vivid memory I want to disappear

no matter how hard I try
no matter how many days go by
no matter how hard I cry
no matter how many lonely nights
I can't get you off my mind
even after all this time
I still long for the girl I now hate
if only I could wish you away

I may never ever see your face
or never ever hear your voice
I may never ever touch your skin
or never ever feel complete
but I'll never ever forget you
or never ever forgive you
I'll never forget you
but I'll never forgive you

no matter how hard I try
no matter how many days go by
no matter how hard I cry
no matter how many lonely nights
I can't get you off my mind
even after all this time
I still long for the girl I now hate
if only I could wish you away

I want you but I don't want you back.

"HATRED IN OUR EYES"

Months turn into years so quickly
the last words that we shared were so angry
you went your way and I went mine
maybe someday we'll say goodbye
without hatred in our eyes

act as if you're not alone
I know you're lying
take some time to regain control
no need for crying
take away
everything you gave
suffocate me
cause you can't break me

minutes turn into hours and so on
I haven't seen you in so long
you have your life and I have mine
maybe some night we'll share the sky
without hatred in our eyes

act as if you're not alone
I know you're lying
take some time to regain control
no need for crying
take away
everything you gave
suffocate me
cause you can't break me

seconds seem to drag on forever
remembering times we spent together
but you have moved on and so have I
I just thought a talk would be nice
without hatred in our eyes

act as if you're not alone
I know you're lying
take some time to regain control
no need for crying
take away
everything you gave
suffocate me
cause you can't break me

I always wanted things to work out
but I know that we are better off now
I just want you to know the truth
so maybe we can meet up soon
I always wanted things to work out
but I know that we are better off now
I just want you to know the truth
so maybe I can see you again soon

act as if you're not alone
I know you're lying
take some time to regain control
no need for crying
take away
everything you gave
suffocate me
cause you can't break me

just a moment of your time is all I ask
so we can finally let go of the past
and put out this hatred in our eyes.

"A KILLER IN ME"

I'll take a drag of this cigarette
laced with cyanide
today is one I won't forget
the end of time
I'll wash it down with a cup of alcohol
to drown your lies
and soon enough I won't feel anything at all
my fatal sacrifice
and I feel my soul leave my body
it's too late now these angels got me
and they carry me to the sky

you're a ticking time bomb in my heart
counting down the seconds till you blow me apart
you used to be the only thing I need
but you've become a lethal killer in me
you're a ticking time bomb in my heart
counting down the seconds till you blow me apart
you used to be the only thing I need
but you've become a lethal killer in me

I'll take a walk to the edge of nowhere
a pristine paradise
to see if I can find some closure there
to free my mind
I'll take a drive off the highest cliff
to the crashing tide
swallow me whole cause I won't be missed
my final suicide
and I feel my soul leave my body
it's too late now these angels got me
and they carry me to the sky

you're a ticking time bomb in my heart
counting down the seconds till you blow me apart
you used to be the only thing I need
but you've become a lethal killer in me
you're a ticking time bomb in my heart
counting down the seconds till you blow me apart
you used to be the only thing I need
but you've become a lethal killer in me

you sent this poison running through my veins
you took my life with all the games you played
but from you I am saved
from you I am saved
you sent this poison running through my veins
you took my life with all the games you played
but from you I am saved
from you I am saved

you're a ticking time bomb in my heart
counting down the seconds till you blow me apart
you used to be the only thing I need
but you've become a lethal killer in me
you're a ticking time bomb in my heart
counting down the seconds till you blow me apart
you used to be the only thing I need
but you've become a lethal killer in me

these angels carry me to the sky
and they'll never hurt me like you did.

"CHANCES WITH KISSES"

You're the last thing on my mind as I close my eyes
lead me to sleep where we are together all night
you're the first thing on my mind as I open my eyes
I've got to make you see, got to make you realize
today could be the first day of our lives
we could be together for the rest of all time

I'll say those words you'll never hear
I'll say those words, scream them loud and clear
so you and everyone will know how I feel
I'll say those words you don't expect
I'll say those words as I kiss your neck
so you and I can make this dream real

boyfriend, what's a boyfriend when there's just you and me
you can't explain but you can't deny our chemistry
you complicate but tantalize my sanity
you leave me hoping, leave me wanting, you are all I need
today could be the day you're finally within reach
we could start forever if you just let yourself believe

I'll say those words you'll never hear
I'll say those words, scream them loud and clear
so you and everyone will know how I feel
I'll say those words you don't expect
I'll say those words as I kiss your neck
so you and I can make this dream real

there's an aching in my stomach that I must satisfy
but I won't be complete until you tell me that you're mine
there's a burning that won't go away inside my chest
you're the only one who can put it out with your kiss
there's an aching in my stomach that I must satisfy
but I won't be complete until you tell me that you're mine
there's a burning that won't go away inside my chest
you're the only one who can put it out with your kiss

I'll say those words you'll never hear
I'll say those words, scream them loud and clear
so you and everyone will know how I feel
I'll say those words you don't expect
I'll say those words as I kiss your neck
so you and I can make this dream real

I'm crying out my final plea
just say that you love me
give me a chance to sweep you off your feet
just say that you love me
cause I do love you.

"THESE HANDS"

There's just something about this town
that keeps beating me to the ground
I'm slipping further from the sound
as these hands are reaching to pull me down
there's just something about this place
that keeps me repeating the same mistakes
I'm finally climbing to escape
but these hands are clawing at my face

never thought it would come to this
but you've been pushed passed your limits
sanity is at your fingertips
but you can't grasp it
never thought it would come to this
but you've been pushed passed your limits
sanity is at your fingertips
but you can't grasp it

there's just something about this night
that keeps draining me of life
I'm fading slowly out of sight
as these hands are digging into my thighs
there's just something about this dark
that keeps piercing into my heart
I'm crying louder than I thought
cause these hands are tearing me apart

never thought it would come to this
but you've been pushed passed your limits
sanity is at your fingertips
but you can't grasp it
never thought it would come to this
but you've been pushed passed your limits
sanity is at your fingertips
but you can't grasp it

I'll set this whole thing ablaze
let it burn till nothing remains
to end the torment coursing through my veins
I'll set this whole thing ablaze
let it burn till nothing remains
to end the torment coursing through my veins

never thought it would come to this
but you've been pushed passed your limits
sanity is at your fingertips
but you can't grasp it
never thought it would come to this
but you've been pushed passed your limits
sanity is at your fingertips
but you can't grasp it

this is the point where heaven meets hell
though which is which I can not tell.

"CHANGE DOESN'T ALWAYS COME EASY"

You want to see who is in my bed
cause it's still me that is in your head
but you've killed everything in my heart
it's bitter cold and it will rip you apart
and everything I've seen
pales in comparison to what I've been through
and even though you're sitting next to me
you're just a ghost of the girl I'm used to

pretty girl don't cry for me
pretty girl don't cry
pretty girl don't die for me
pretty girl don't die
jealousy's just a frame of mind
that you have to fight to survive
and honesty's buried under lies
keep them coming if you wanna get out alive

you want to dig deeper than before
but you've dug too deep now you're scraping the core
you want to peel the layers of my skin
but you cut right through this masquerade I've been
and everything we were
leaves me with a stale and bitter taste
and even though you're sitting next to me
you're just a ghost of the girl I once chased

pretty girl don't cry for me
pretty girl don't cry
pretty girl don't die for me
pretty girl don't die
jealousy's just a frame of mind
that you have to fight to survive
and honesty's buried under lies
keep them coming if you wanna get out alive

change doesn't always come easy
when you're not used to being alone
and love sometimes feels more like cancer
when injected it's infecting our bones
change doesn't always come easy
when you're not used to being alone
and love sometimes feels more like cancer
when injected it's infecting your bones

pretty girl don't cry for me
pretty girl don't cry
pretty girl don't die for me
pretty girl don't die
jealousy's just a frame of mind
that you have to fight to survive
and honesty's buried under lies
keep them coming if you wanna get out alive

pretty girl we're not worth saving
pretty girl our love is decaying
pretty girl it's not worth trying
cause breathing never felt so much like dying
like dying
like dying
LIKE DYING
like dying
breathing never felt so much like dying.

The End!!!

www.ingramcontent.com/pod-product-compliance
Lightning Source LLC
Chambersburg PA
CBHW032038150426

43194CB00006B/325